SELECTED AND
NEW POEMS

To all my family, past and present

JOHN POWELL WARD

SELECTED AND
NEW POEMS

To Graham and Ann
all best wishes and love,

John Powell Ward
May 2004

seren

Seren is the book imprint of
Poetry Wales Press Ltd
Nolton Street, Bridgend, Wales
www.seren-books.com

The right of John Powell Ward to be identified as the
Author of this Work has been asserted in accordance with
the Copyright, Designs and Patents Act, 1988.

ISBN 1-85411-346-1
A CIP record for this title is available from the British Library.

The publisher acknowledges the financial assistance
of the Welsh Books Council.

Printed by Bell & Bain, Glasgow.

Cover image a detail of 'Matted' (1994) by Tim Davies
(feathers, sump oil; photographed by Graham Matthews).

Contents

Early Uncollected Poems

from *The Other Man* (1969)

from *To Get Clear* (1981)

from *The Clearing* **(1984)**

from *A Certain Marvellous Thing* **(1993)**

from *Genesis* **(1996)**

from *Late Thoughts in March* **(1999)**

Later Uncollected and New Poems

Early Uncollected Poems

Coming to Live

The village then. The sun
Slants on my door, soon could be set my part.
The shop, the green – the land here has
No proof, no questioning; a bird's note
Chips the silence and a car cuts by.

Old iron stranded in the stream
Is motionless. Like that dead tree.
Your half-smile, was it recognition? I
Alighted as a stranger, yet
You knew me, that I worked in town,
Was gone by bus in the morning....

Every eye notched up the arrival. What's
This acre's secret, what instructs
The wagging dog, inching my hand?
                                    "Nothing
You need to know" they say, "just let your chimney
Hoist its smoke now like the rest". And so I do,
Not in distress, nor hope, just another man
Senseless of God beneath the church's croft
Or the clear, unwritten, ink-blue card of sky.

Tintagel

The sensitive would call its shattered size pathetic.
But families below, scribbled where the cove corrodes,
Sunbathe face-down, indifferent; still against its sides
The old sea bangs in boredom, dumps trunks in the attic.

Most others (Windsor currently in favour) impress
As photogenic from the air, preserve their past
In high-hung canvas, cardboard models, unswept dust;
Not numinous; *objets* though, pieces for chess.

Not so here. Here no showmanship but silence,
No further comment. Footpaths like chewed string,
                                        golf courses,
Sun avuncular, sky of teapots and blue roses;
A rounded elevation from sea-level, an expanse.

Evening admittedly, hurrying out the camera crowd
At closing time in timeless fingerprints of grey
Pleases the grey heads, lingering on steps; on the way
Children pick the walls to see if they would bleed;

But lovers have to glance behind for reasons of their own.
The sunset lights dark candles, whispers to the rocks
To kneel, perhaps; Tintagel, embarrassed by such hoax,
Blushes back the red into the west. For this began

Bare; before its past unbuilt (as it is nearly now)
Feudal, harsh; and thanks for its once new then
                                        mellowed beauty
A king's perceptions of defence, castled capacity
For *his* age. So, all done, do guide-books cling for more?

Forget it. On to morning, plead for an eyesore,
Bungalows, anything; just bury this. See those cliffs loom
Out chalk artillery, and waves like newsprint bring a
                                        new theme,
Developments, or (irrelevant here) a new war.

Ernest Morgan's House

This was Ernest Morgan's house. Today
It is his skull, the crawling crowd
Has got in through the cracks, loads hall
And stairs, spills out of windows, eating
His home's breath from the highest corner. Aloof
Is the belted truth of the auctioneer; they swarm
Right past him, they want secrets of
The realm an old recluse had left, who thought
He had no friend, or needed none, or had
None left he needed. They do it like this:
Chasing a form whose absence let them in,
Jamming rooms he'd sat in, bolt, alone,
Gorging themselves on voids his leaving left.
Then they go home. Suns sets, the worm
Works on in Ernest Morgan's grave.

Walk-on Part

Silence suffuses. Actors
Have left to get drunk, people
Drive snugwards. Curtains,
Wide open, stress a difference,
The stuffed stage and the empty
Auditorium below. Yet
Not quite silence. Silence, draped
On the flies, on the mike,
Is not quite silence. An old man
Is moving, distinctly. His broom
Knocks the tubular chairs. His mien
Is jobless. Someone
Of import got him here, someone
Less nameless than himself. A spotlight,
Now off, quietly mocks. He scuffs
Old programmes with his bristles. His eyes
Are lowered from the stage. Himself,
His role, prominence bought with
Unique self-exposal; he's too
Part of that, where he's standing.

One brief time, centre stage, he looks up,
Draws breath, turns, and faces
The dark and receding abyss, the black setting
Identity's act never sees yet
Performs to. You could hear a pin drop.

                Bent double
Again he sweeps, crippling his back
But a man still. Round and behind him
Rows of seats stare, the high ceiling
Echoes, with vanished applause.

from *The Other Man* (1969)

The Burglar

I lock all the doors each night, I lock
Off separate rooms, I seal the house
As tight as glue about me, force
Myself to try and sleep; still in the dark
The whole thing isn't mine; I think,

I hear the clock, next to that a chink
Of noise below from one who's in, who knows
His way like I do; stands and stops and goes
Like I do; link by link
Dismantling treasure till each shelf is bare

Then straight back to the night, where the black air
Shuts like a gate behind him into place.
I think of day, the sun's beat on my face.
I toss and turn till morning. Don't ask me where
He's from, or why I've never loved
The things he steals, or why I don't compare
Him to myself. I know one thing:
At night he comes, I hear him working there.

A Churchyard

Still nothingness tonight. Over the wall
A black and bottomless pit, for the night was black
And the lamp in the road was behind me – all

I saw was dark, no imaginable eye
Could tell even stones from tufts of grass,
Let alone the way the resting corpses lie.

And the struggle still; how to say it. How in the day
The tombs float lazily clear in a slack
High noon; how at night what they

Contain rides out of mortal sight, beyond
These harrying stars that pierce the sky, the wind
That roars on the bridge and pulls

The tree-tops; still the small words trudge on
Like a tramp, keeping low to the ground
Through intricate lanes that wind nowhere but back
To the deep-dug hole in the earthwork

They came from; mute, irretrievably gone.

The Two Travellers

in they got, shutting the door with
a smack, just as the train pulled out.
we sat in silence, watching them.

and they sat too, taut as posts, with their
bowler hats, pin-stripes, briefcases.
all flow of words, of thought, they stifled.

they seemed to permeate, the two of them,
the entire compartment. they wouldn't talk, didn't
smoke, must have the windows open.

like identical twins they sat. same
attire, same expression of uprightness,
stiffness. they seemed to require each other.

and us, too. there was no refreshment,
no slouching in the corridor. they'd
trapped us, here in our seats, and we sat still.

then the station came. with sudden energy they
left, to our relief. I glimpsed their names,
Time and Space, engraved on their cases.

Every Single Night

I get into bed.
A man climbs carefully in
Through a hole in my head.

He sweeps out a pile
Of straw, and lies down. The moon
Illumines his smile.

He's filthily dressed –
A squashed bowler and striped
Butcher's trousers. A clown's, almost?

His manner appears
To ignore (though perceiving)
My presence. Why me? Christ knows.

He sleeps soundly. We share
All I own; he the boards, me the blankets.
By dawn he's not there.

Does he hear me here, cursing the poor?
But I don't. They never occur
To my mind at all.

Does he think of me, tossing, awake
On his account? I can't
Answer. He doesn't speak.

Will he never have reason to go?
No more than for coming, I'd have
Thought, though by nature, can't know.

What nature have I,
When a tramp's got the grind
Of the world in his own

Rotting skull, and sets up like a lord in mine?

Poem Outside Woolworth's

Images all at once.
Criss-cross lines in the flags
Of concrete, solid beneath
The flippant chrome that hangs
Unasked round fat women's bags.

Halitosis, chattering breath.
Rows of jars marked 'Off'.
The whole building, ugly, being
The town's particular wealth
For a general combine. Stuff

You need every day. Cruising
Up in price. Bumping the crowds
To hell round muck on view
While lorries clumsily bring
Tons more to the backs of the yards.

A packet of needles, a new
Pair of stockings, a bicycle part.
Astride the mountains of goods
Is a Woolworth girl in blue.
I adore her, with all my heart.

Something

Something streaks in at us like morning sun,
Too precious to compare with the dingy stuff
Already on the shelves, and we hardly dare
To call it ours; yet it comes in of itself,
In the house, the room, an actual thing that belongs;
It gets into our hands and we feel it there.

And then we drop it; we, or me, or something else
Not in ourselves that plays us false
As dirt and makes us hold too tight,
Until we pull all wrong and curse and hate –
Then stop and look, aghast; it doesn't matter,
We've spoilt the thing, thinking we both knew better;

And back we go, more slowly, edging our way,
Stumbling at every foothold, trying to reach
A place to talk from, trying to catch
The tiniest glimpse of what we'd grabbed
And lost; how hard and real it looked, how strong.
Was it a diamond? We search all day
Till nightfall, under the desk, the chairs,
Through carpeted rooms and up the stairs; surely
It must be around, what bound us so close together.
But we find nothing there, except each other.

Fin De Siecle

Light flickers quick in the trees
In the boulevard, morning and bread
Get daily delivered to cafés and doors
Unknowingly opened. A soft fresh breeze
Stirs the maples. The king is dead.

The day matures, the sun abhors
No mode of itself, it rises lying
Square in the sky till bodies can't stand
The heat of a dispossessed noon; scores
Feel the shift in the kidney. A people are dying.

Streets stand, empty. The millennial pause
At dusk for the one child crying.
History's surgeon stares across the land.

Borderline Cases are Coloured

You don't understand
sir. Paragraph four says a white
person is one who is clearly and
obviously white, or recognized as
such, by other whites.
A coloured person is one
who is not white. A white
person may not be recognized as
coloured unless there is proof that
he is, in fact, coloured.
A coloured person can *never* be
recognized as white, since if
he were white he could never
have been recognized as coloured.
Borderline cases are coloured: a
recognized white may defend
himself against the charge of
being borderline. His pigments
will be analysed, his ancestry
investigated, his hair
tested for wire-fuzz by running
it through with a ball-point. Whites
being white there is nothing
to fear from such investigation of
whites by whites

from *To Get Clear* (1981)

On the Lake

And he sat, silent as water,
in the stern, a bare rug on his
knees, and a dead perch on the
thwart, dark hills a circling
audience for the fish's eye,
staring up, at the night's expanse
above, and at hills, and a tiny
village and Post Office black on
the shore, and he drew his oars
from the water with no sound, the
blades' flat surfaces themselves
wet pools, and the lake's
tremendous tilt, to the naked
hills, and he eased another fish,
from the rod's barb, and it
glimmered, and at that moment,
he flicked his rod, from behind him,
and it went up, and the apex of
its cast, touched the North Star,
then fell, past Sirius, past the
meeting of black sky and hills,
sliced into two a farmhouse and
its milking-sheds, sliced down
through clumps of deciduous trees
and oaks, and a stone well, into
the lake, and the rod's needle-
point, pricked the water's surface,
and he waited, and rowed a
silent stroke, and three drops fell
from the oars' arms, and lay like
tiny lakes on the gunwales, and the
rollocks' joints squelched, and he
waited, and he and the hills and
the level lake, passed the night,
while on those hills' further side,
another lake lay, a smaller silver
tree-lined lake, staring up from
the hills' timber, like a fish's eye.

Bristol Channel

Meditation and water are wedded forever. – Melville

Or any coast…. Miles out a white
Wave rolls in the distance like a whale's
Belly showing. A single tip
Of white vanishes like a far ship
Going down. There are nicks and falls
Of white so far out at sea they seem
No more than notion or idea of foam,
A nail-paring. A pale hand seems to wave
Then fade, like a riding-lamp seems to give
One beam then not be, a lace
Curtain's corner falls back into place.

Another wave's a sheet laundering.
One like a bar extends its length
And not alone. Through binoculars
Its folding follower jumps in close.
Seek nakedly, small again, but coming.
The next seems like the first's new try.
I could look forever, as out there an eye
Does at me, each wave making
New sense, breaking yet not exactly breaking
And soothing the sand's weak brow because
Wave's work is rough as no man's is.

Men once thought it was horses out there,
Or a voice singing. You could say so.
Now I cognize a watery shape
Of horse as made by Proteus's deep
And primal as any white-tipped mare.
Beyond, Homer's highway of fishy fins
Up and down channel in sixteen lanes
Permits such legend, cutting across
The tide's direction, drilling its course
Sending wave on wave in just to you,
Thinker. It comes in just for you.

The Guards

Thou hast made us for Thyself... – St Augustine

We get a stock of bees for food.
I concentrate, yet am afraid
Of options gone, there's always been
Distraction. What is that thing,
The dark thing certainly not wrong
That holds the centre and from which
All our attentions always switch?

The swarm drops on the laid-out cloth.
A few crawl to the wooden fort
We left; the hive. We watch. Untaught
Then like a moving heap of earth
They take possession of that tang
And waxy place. Then ten weeks from
Their slit the mindless workers come

For pollen masticated crude
For young in each sealed loaded cell.
Then swarm. Invaders are destroyed.
Drones die purged on the landing-sill.
On time in gauntlets and a veil
I sugar where ten thousand live
And take the lid up from the hive.

A detail of the bees swings up
And peels off left to get me. Dip,
Savage the gloves, sting leather in
Their suicidal ire and die.
In suit and net and warily
I thieve their honey-frames by hand,
Vats of brown liquid churned like sand.

What do they guard, with this fierce work,
Vibrating so hard those weak wings
Directing scent? We puff more smoke.
The brood chamber is black as hell.
But who and what you are, wee queen,
Eludes still, like my childhood, clean
As me decked out in this white shell.

Genes

A duet of boys.
Limbs, sticks of the species.
Chubby and spindly knees,
No nail yet on their brows.

This fair one is loved
For his forgiving.
I could not do it, have
Such pensive

Clearance in an oval face.
The opal eyes
Accept that he felt no cause
For hurts he willingly allows,

My wood-shaving, my tiny wisp of straw.
Some man years later
May rise from a chair
And tread carpet to you, lead you

Astray, his wants to answer.
Then we'll remember
The light on your puzzled hair,
My ash-leaf, our sliver of a tree.

Darker, tiny one,
What you seem to contain
Is flesh as wit, new-laid comedian.
You looked like a laughing moon

In bouncing back light
Too young to snatch it
Like a ball, to we who pat it.
For your subtler shape we must wait

Then, little egg, fat moonlight.
And if such boys are our contract
In blood, one fair one dark
And both gene mystery, how do we act

Who do not even know
Whence they came, what miracle they imply?
In our eyes prayer
Is impossible; of course we try.

Winter

I see across the fields a whole
Flock of sheep being rounded up
By a dog. It looks from
Here like a black slug, it lies so
Flat on the snow. Then darts
Through the hedge, a shiny but skilled
Black streak across the white. Then I see
A five-barred gate in front of
Those fields, angular against
Those fields. And there's
The agricultural man, making
Little I dare say from this
Well-fed but tiny flock, yellow-grey
Across the white, the sheet white
Of that field. And if I walk to my cottage
Curving the corner of the hilly
Lane still white with unridden snow, and I
A scholar get back to my room, then I'll
Look out at the snow and then back at
The cool white pages on my
Desk, pages of snow and the
Mysterious black streaks upon them.

The Word-hoard

When the man died devoid of will
We found his cabinets of print
In the oast-house. They stood arranged
In a tall circle like Stonehenge
Of the big thighs, and one weak light,
Low from the crossbeams on a cord,
Made tiny shadows down each word,
Resetting them. Everything said
Ten million sentences in lead.

Eight-foot cabinets with drawers
Flat as for maps or seamen's charts.
Damp tried to cool my head and sleeve,
This rondel going Aladdin's cave
Awhile. We picked out palpable
Print scattered absently by him,
Our fingers sifting like a dream
In milk if milk's velvet to touch.
I never loved a thing so much.

Every drawer labelled: Spartan Bold,
Bodoni, Goudy, Charlemagne.
Neuland is like the Maltese cross.
Times serifs tapered like a wine
As delicate as whiskered hair,
It nearly moved. Everywhere
Was junk and blocks for Christmas cards
And names and one Madonna and child.
All the texts mirrored in reverse,

Our ultimate talent of mind.
If I were placed to guarantee
My feeble brain's materials,
Writer's materials, they'd be
As weird as this, as mad, the amount
And types of type, small squiggles, tanned
Birds, margins, stars grease-tipped to shine,
As though man's knowledge born of print
Regressed from such designing. Wrapped

As we retired I found mint new
The tiniest alphabet, silver
In hue and caught my breath in awe.
A lettered necklace for your love!
How are these icons consummate
In cast so potent? The pen-stroke's curve
Arrested tights grips the word-hoard
Back into rock, then ink from it
Slenders our blood. Some brief small thing

Like "flesh made word" bears uttering.
Yet here next week another man
Must re-appear to melt it down
Back to base lead Bassanio chose,
Winning his tempt. Outside thin rain,
Tapping its upright keys on hills,
Drops gentle dew from heaven. The best
I take friends, and thus in my fist
Hammer-head weights bear down decay.

BP Llandarcy

Blue, olive, pink, buff, chocolate-brown.
A railway train of cottages.

Black crows flap past a wrecked car.
Sheep graze in precious space.

The bare chapel preserves its shape.
No chimney or aerial, just its shape.

Mam scrubs and scrubs, a child recoils.
Dogs fight in the washing-line.

Beyond, on a hilltop:
Two colossal kilns, a pilot flame
And storage tanks settling from the sky
Like flying saucers; pylons as priests.
A chimney points smoke vertically
Sacrificing minerals with uplifted hands.

Each era's fiction ends up on the hill.
We breathe its silt and sediment.

Two Events Near Loyola

The car wound steeply down the hairpin trail,
The valleys' deep fields hazed with mustard, kale.

We reached a speckled village halfway down
With hovels but a massive church. We should go in.

A tiny wrist pulled at the heavy lock.
The latch moved with a huge, explosive click.

Nothing stirred, except the altar's flame.
Priest and kneeler quivered the godhead's name.

We crossed the square, sun-blazed, a moment after,
And found a pipe, and from its iron mouth, water.

We wallowed in it, slaked it on our hair,
Wrung out our shirts, spun wet drops through the air.

Not just watch-hands told the time to go.
Seconds later, vast valleys lay below.

The Party

And finally the garden and
terrace were finished, and they
decided on a party, with salads, cheese
and a bowl of strawberries, and Peter
and Sue came down the steps with a
bottle of wine and some mushrooms, and
others came, and they had a fat
trestle table, with dinner-plates with
cold meats on, ham, salami, chicken
and some pork, and on an old pub
table beside it, on the lawn edge,
were tomatoes cut into eighths, and
Jim and Hanna came next with their
unmarried aunt, and two or three
groups stood with a fork and paper
napkins in each hand, and a glass of
either red or rose wine, or tomato
juice, and some had already entered
the cold apple pie, fruit from trees
on the wall, and there was potato
salad, celery, lettuce, and cress from
the stream, and some cold trout, smooth
on the tongue like butter, and all
the eaters stood, not sat, and Frank
was able to pick a rose-petal, and a
whole rose, waist high, with oil-covered
fingers, where the terrace's slabs
met the lawn, and Shirley spoke to
Martin, handing him a slice of tongue,
and a cold mushroom salad was then
brought out, and shellfish done with
larger cod in a cheese sauce, and a
child played on the terrace's slabs
with a wheel, looking like a radish
itself, and the apple pie's crust went
slowly up and down, and the juice made

it soggy, and cream licked it, and a
lean dapper man pushed two sardines
with his fork, and with a cube of
bread in its oil, and Donald and Diana
came late, were uncertain but gave a
cask of ginger, and they finished some
uncut cucumber, tomatoes and lettuces,
and very crusty bread before the one
plum pie as well as the three apple
pies, and by then the men were in
threes talking, the girls eating savoury
biscuits and cheese also with the men,
both in some cases, and the champagne
was in some cases, and George put his
plate of Camembert and Brie, and
strawberries, down on the terrace's
slabs for a minute, smiling to the
child to avoid it, and gave Jane some
more cream and red wine in a glass like
a tulip, at the slab's edge, and
I made this into a poem, for poetry is
a necessity, as is food.

London Welsh v. Bridgend

Then I got on the train, very late
at night, Saturday, and lay on the seat,
exhausted, as did the other man
there, a little man, beady-eyed and
with a pointed chin, and he pulled the
blinds down, and we lay, and just about
dozed off when bam! door opened,
in came half a rugby team, enormous
fellows, tipped me off the seat on the
filthy floor, then sat down, singing,
shouting, crashing on each other with
their beer cans, and one sat by the
beady man, running his fingers exquisitely
along the fellow's thigh-bone, through
his trousers, but in only a bawdy
way, friendly even, if you could believe
it, and they roughed, and one
arse in the corridor, undid the fire
extinguisher, soaked us, and another
slammed the door, sat down again, kept
asking me the beady man's name, which
I didn't know, angry now, afraid even,
but decided to be sensible, and got
going, talked, had their beer, and they
got serious to meet me, a most
generous gesture, and a big man, older
than the others, kept deflecting the
attention, of the bawdy one from the
beady one, the bawdy one trying to make
the beady one talk, which he couldn't,
in inhibition, and cringing fear, and I
felt sorry, but leant on the carriage arm,
with them, drinking, singing, yawning, and
hearing about his wife, from one of them,
till, at last, they were quieter, they had
won their match, they had had a good day,

and they dozed off, one on my shoulder, sixteen
stone, snoring loudly, but I finally dozed
off, at the train's rhythm, rattling
through the darkness, and I half-woke,
at times, saw a misty scene, as of Arthur's
knights, brief white faces, assembled,
swaying, then dozed, felt the train stop
in my half-asleep condition, and men get
out, a shrieking porter, and banging doors,
then slept again, and then woke, two
hundred miles from London; they had
all gone, every one, bar the beady one, and I
sat, heavy, soggy, wanting lukewarm tea, and
saw, with my round eye and my mind's eye,
the aftermath of dawn, and the mess of the
twentieth century; the industry, the steel
works and the smelting works, a new day, for
better or worse in our hands, and the
carriage window, filthy, but a filter,
for that streaky, watery, nearly
light-blue, blue.

Before Experience

We toiled all day
Bare to the waist, sweating
With the rocks for dray.

Bulletins told
Of far-away governments,
Promises, Wall Street oversold.

The waves broke
On the shore and salt-thick
Wood lay uncollected, bespoke.

On the shore
Was object-matter; tarred rope, ropes,
Seaweed oiled by different work before.

What did we need? To say
"Our spirits ate, we were the nourishers,
We were not unsustained today."

I lay later, in bed,
Dreamt of the child and the starving man
Dreaming of bread.

Platonic Immersion

We leave the chlorine, rub us down
With soap, then feel a steaming film
Of sweat so tacky none can dry.
The towel's nap wettens and we learn
Where were invincibility,
Desire and pleasure, three in one.
All three broke up the waters' calm.

The good and beautiful and true.
Young men rip towels across their backs
Like stropping off their muscles' wit,
And Aqualung exponents view
A friend's refracted silhouette,
Frogging the tiles below the blue,
Going at the diving brick he seeks,

While female athletes rail the side,
Soak each pore and deploy strong breasts,
Cleaving their liquid's double bulge.
Tall bodies leave the diving-board,
Feet high behind, legs like a wedge
In scintillating entry. Freud
Who inked our thought's wet in, suggests

These third moats are natality;
In this expensive college pool,
Not double-scotch-and-splash, or gin,
But water, laved abundantly
Immediate, contacting skin,
Makes safe such wallowing and free.
As more bath empties, we slake still.

A last wet body climbs out, dried.
Closure of *balneae* of Rome.
Blue racing-lanes calm down, and deep
Waves lilt and lop against the side,
Heave gently like a child asleep,
Its stirring done. We swimmers glide
Outdoors and go our three ways home.

Down the Moor

they still run wild on the Gower peninsula

One moves, her foal a yard behind
Grazing against the mare. To eat
Is soft embodiment of thought,
Turf's sponge was all their feed. The foal's
Knees look like spindly cotton reels,
And canter cautiously. One had
My apple. Lips, a suction pad,

Collapsed the red lump in its mouth.
Twenty-five horses move as one,
Their manes across their backs like brown
Dead bracken, nostrils almond-holed.
I never saw a thing less wild.
They drift like tips of breeze, I wish
My own thought came as cleanly such.

A head like glancing silk is turned,
A girl's hand waving. Flares of gorse
All round the motion of the horse
Blaze it out often, like the day.
One shambles suddenly away
Seeing the car, then pauses with
My pocket in its eyes, the mouth

Shut wetly. When the whole herd leaves
The moorland as the instinct comes,
They all go off at different times.
One moves a bit, two more graze, stop
Then follow, then to ground they drop
Their heads most naturally. Barely more
Than thought they move off down the moor.

Here, Home

I got home, very late, and parked the
car, by the hedge, and entered the porch,
and was turning the key, when I heard a
single fox bark, a mile away, and I went
inside, put down my suitcase, and spread
my fingers on the wall to find the light-
switch, and one bulb lit dimly, and the
terrier, lying on the carpet, opened one
eye, after a second's pause, and then, a
little later, he seemed, gradually, to be
moving, and raising himself, on rear legs
only, and then the front, with an effort,
and then walked, rather slowly, about five
steps, to me, where his nose stopped, barely
a quarter inch, from my trouser-leg, where
he stood, in a kind of acknowledgement, as
it were, and my fingers touched his wire
head, and I heard, a very tiny breathing, as
of two small people, perhaps, and at the top,
of the stairs, a bedroom door, half-opened,
yielded a cot, with a still form, what I
knew to be, tousled sheets, and one half of
a small, curly head of hair, exposed, like
an object I perceived, or was expert on,
and a little body, under the sheets, which
went up, and then back, so carefully, and
I walked, still with my overcoat, on, along
the passage, past another bedroom, in which
a bigger boy slept, so strongly, and a further door,
also, was open, to its bedroom, where a
wife lay, in black pyjamas, asleep, the
face loaded, very full, but pre-empted for
the night, and by her, in the double bed,
was a space, the shape and size of a man,
into which I climbed, fitting it, exactly,
and lay half-asleep, templating it, or would
seem so, to a further fox or man who arrived.

from *The Clearing* (1984)

The Old Man Sailing

He had to sail, he had to take his car
On Saturdays down to the water's edge
  And row

His dinghy with his scarlet biscuit-tins
Of weekend food out to his rusty boat
  And climb

Aboard to nutty ropes in lockers in
The cabin, then go up the steps on deck
  And see

The north-west breeze (force 3) he always liked
Just agitate the water, hoist the jib
  And swing

Off his cream moorings; further down the tide
He'd up the mainsail by himself, all this
  And yet

He couldn't swim a stroke, home had to be
The sea, conscience
  And wrist

In pleasure's grip or let his young crew have
A go, his smile so happy as they drowned
  And swam.

After the Conference

"How is society possible?" – Georg Simmel

We left the motorway, rolled west
At dusk and prudently refilled
Our tanks and minds, England had passed
To night when Wales came finally.
After Leominster we made Hay
And flicked the wheel, gestured as if
The quilts of fields were light relief.
Or signified a normal world.

A sharper gradient changed the play
Of steering where the road ascends.
"Our era thinks humanity
Is nothing but each other; we
Are types and groups exclusively."
Great theme for a conference.
Past Brecon's river-confluence
We climb; low hills, then hairpin bends.

A stunted thorn tree slips away
In gleamless mountains. We go up,
A moment awed and nearly pray
The fan-belt won't slip loose or nut
Work free. An electric light,
Repairman's shack, shines from the vale's
Deep cleavage. Then the road-edge falls
Sheer off; height-sick we reach the top,

Brake, and get out. So still.... The grass
Is midnight grey, a car goes by,
Speeding its geometry of stars.
Far below the farmyards hang.
Up here is space, air almost nothing.
Alarmingly a single bird
Cheeps, hatching stones, one note repeated.
We gaze up at infinity,

The lack of life there. Leo pads
His hind-paw Alpha-Regulus
By space-time round the Crab and fades
To Gemini. I feel two-fifths the size
Of one speck on the windscreen, years
And days diminish, peak divides
Get crossed. Back in, and gathering speed,
We pick out well below the pass

A tiny settlement, as seen
From jets at altitude; a flare
Of lights or elfin ring; Hirwaun's
Industrial camp. Viewed from up here
Wales never was less secular.
"Where is this place?" How's an appraisal
Possible? We coasted on
To Dic's Penderyn, two miles down.

Still Life

And he purchased, a very large green
bottle, of yellow wine, and he took it home, and
he put it on the sideboard, while he cooked veal
with sauté potatoes, and celery, and laid the
table, for himself, and a second place, and he
walked back to the sideboard, and picked up
the silver-plated corkscrew, glinting in the
evening light of the yellow sun, which was
splintering the window's glass, and he held
the bottleneck in his fist, its bottom, and punt
away from him, like a thrusting knife, and he
put the corkscrew's point at exactly the
centre, of the cork's texture, and he pushed
and turned at once, with his palm's heel,
pressing on the handle, and saw candle-light
in the bottle's green glass, and he
pressed, so that the circling spiral, went
into the cork, and then he held the dark green
bottle, contrasting his white hands as it did,
away from him, but with the palm upright, and
held the corkscrew, and pulled very hard, and
there was a satisfying deep noise, and he
sluiced a little wine, into a glass's
transparency, and held it up, by the stem, between
thumb and finger, like a flower, and tasted
it, and put the bottle on the table, so that
its green, and the yellow wine, and the bowl
of green apples and grapes, were together, and
there was a tap at the door, and he straightened
the mat, at the second place he had laid.

Evangelical Upbringing and Covent Garden

Each year we picked; late in the night
Of wine-dark sky we took the fruit
On lorries, and a fork-lift's prongs
Slammed into slits where apples' wrongs
Rolled on a timber platform. Fruit
Was everywhere; green peppers, chaste
Blackcurrants scratchy on the taste

And tasted; oranges in nets
Like fish-catch, cucumbers, courgettes,
Big lime-green melons like the brood
Of some millennial melon-bird;
Aubergines the bland antiques
Of horticulture. From its twig
The pear's obese, low pending sag....

Now, our life has modified.
Fantastic plums have dropped and died.
For we are fruit the wristy hand
Autumnally has gathered and
Re-gathered till our egos rot
And swell to putrefaction; yet
Aren't we the wasps as well, stings drawn?

I take the allegory on
And live with it. Through London's map
We rattled home in streets as ripe
As tyres or skins, a belfry hung
With cherry-bunches no one rang.
Truth was the mind, mine Milton's girl.
Tall acid Eve and what she stole.

At the Pool

We stood there on a winter's day.
The rootless horn-wort often seen
In shallow moorland pools was there,
This pond a spring or watering-hole
For Gower horses. Picked, this weed
Had dangling a tube of slime
Meniscus on its emerald green.
Immersed again it spreads its full
Feathers about in loose relief,
Back in wild, icy water. If

We looked at it, we stared at it
In fact, just like the 'nature class'
That we in some ways have become,
Living out here. Bogweed, starwort,
A long-haired not a spongy moss
We'd never known, its thrilling stems
The legs of centipedes. And this
Was all so tiny. Aren't we so?
Our own three faces loomed above
The oasis in the gorse and thorn.

Sun's cold December face looked down
By ours and found the beetles there.
A thousand of them under ice.
An exhibition under glass.
Tom picked a handful of the mud;
A leggy water-louse was pulled
From weeks of sleep, and came to air
Knowing its moment suddenly.
It nudged and nosed the ooze till Tom
Lowered it gently back, like I

Would settle himself down into bed
At night again, when woken up.
Every jump that insect made
Had human feeling, human verb.

You pressed a hand down on the ice.
A bubble slid beneath across
Like mercury, sword-blades of grass
Sent shadows to the greasy floor
In globules; several beetles moved.
Whirligigs, Tom's brother said.

Such winter and no sound at all.
Where have the creatures gone, their shells?
The tiny decomposing wings
Of damsel-flies? No trace or sign.
Above, a hunter jet alone,
Then two, one miles away, its sound
Pursuing like an open jaw
To swallow men up, like a pike.
What do these microscopic things,
These wee crustaceans know? How can

We say we aren't as them? Our whole
Galactic night a molecule
On some aquatic being's leg
Or hair. I cling to the belief
In something more than human life,
A trillion times ourselves or else
So small no microscope could see
Its skin. A bird clicks, rattles in
The thorn bush, scrapes the air, its throat
A castanet that zips away

Off from its island in this pool
Worn by the horses come to drink
And slice the clay away, each mound
An island. Lines of algae fill
Canadian pondweed's swollen buds.
Our careful faces leave the bugs
Their biosphere and stronger spring,
A bubble underneath each wing
For buoyancy. We walk, blow frost
And God knows what else round the sky.

Dreaming Birds

The eyes and feathers intermesh.
Descartes said birds were small machines.
A startled starling clattered off
And flew away at that, it screeched
That birds are loops in modern minds,
Weird flights, a mode, a fatal curve,
Of values in the air. The thrush

Is proto-sculpture on the lawn,
The SS crow patrolling down
A motorway's hard shoulder struts
At sentry duty. From a pole
A blackbird soloist transmits
Its live performance and the cool
Woods pay to hear him, dark guitars

Are slung there and electric cries
Flash down the alleyways of spruce,
Afforestation's gentlest crop.
The dreamer Kant thought of a dove
That found air fretful, so conceived
A purer flight in empty space.
I dream of swifts that soar asleep.

Evening Bathers

A creamy warm Atlantic thins
And washes up the cockles. Where
The August sun goes down and near
A nervous mother, tiny boys
Adore the swirlings round their knees;
Stick-insects, laughing skeletons.

A surfer leans his thighs to glide
The pink foams to a beaching-place.
A girl stares at the fishing rod
Wedged in the sand. Bent from a catch
The curling tendril makes a snatch
At air. Before a rock's blue face

Last families are cricketing,
Ball sailing like a red-beaked gull
To be caught. The sea's rolled shavings steel
Themselves to come on in. Along
The hedgerow of each blossoming wave
The surfer rides; we divers dive

Under the saline drift for words
Down to a luminous green weed.
Philologies crash overhead
Above our continental shelf,
And waist-deep fathers stare amazed
At orange and the sky itself

To see come catapulting in
The surfer's black cap like a seal.
The evening bathers feel so real
In their mauve caravans tonight.
They watch the huge tomato sun
Drop bouncing on its trampoline.

The Present

for S

We twist our heads out through the bedroom window
And wait. There is night and the blackness under.

There is dew, endless and level, no matter how
The empirical tide has dusted our minds dry now.

There is darkness, and an autumn smell, which no doubt
Humans could easily learn to live without.

It's dark out here; my legs and stomach feel warm,
Though. Is this past night still doing our cheeks harm?

Certainly now we could pull back our heads and say
"You're so real, love, and sex is here to stay."

Certainly we could; and couldn't we once declare
Nature was womb and the big lay everywhere?

An owl hoots. Yes, you can hear them here still.
Time's not a thing, it is we who fill

It seeking an existence where we can belong.
Is sniffing a leaf, in nineteen-eighty, wrong?

Asking, we pull our heads back in from the darkness.
There's dew on your hair. You undress.

Them

i

I kiss the sleeping kid,
my face so close to his,
see past the open mouth
yielding and tiny pores.
His skin is grubby white
as I regard, and yet
fearing myself. Too close
emotion seeds from this-size love.

I love his bullet head
And want to touch his skin.
The orbiting room-air
Encircles quietly as
I love him and love him.
With no task he came
Awhile, bringing his life.
I daren't make a sound.

ii

Our elder, blond boy,
carrying an axe by its
head in January and

a chain-saw for me. We both
remember the crackle of ice
in the cow's deep hock-prints

and chips of ash
as we swung the haft
over our heads.

He would look across at
where a heron flapped slowly
up from a pool like

a masked executioner;
he incarnates patience, quiet;
he stares at a wet

drop on wood for minutes.
I watch our jewel holding,
holding its price.

Calvin

*Faith in predestination is merely the
final consequence of faith in the grace
of Christ in the presence of the enigmas
of experience.* – Paul Wernle.

Conversion is reverse of thaw,
Green patches disappearing; snow
Dropped like a hand of God on fields,
On filth. Order I'd bring
To all detail of everything.

I stare out at the dazzling snow.
It made a mirror of the sky
And purity; I was deceived
At first till later truth improved
To certainty, came as I loved.

Destined for blackness and coal's hell,
In chains clank on the reprobate.
Our pleased designer of the law
Cannot do wrong, nor frees one man
Presumed for such. God's black is white

As this deep snow falling at night.
Insects congest beneath the bridge
Of his fat shoe where we are crushed
Or chosen. Black is beautiful,
And most are damned before they live

And live responding; saying thus
Must clarity we want embrace
Outdating 'moral', 'good' and 'right',
So come mysteriously like love,
The final consequence of faith,

Dull liberals avoiding eyes.
Science, Marx, progress are this way.
I have this icicle of thought.
I shall not pluralize the white.
There is no fear in what I say.

The Beaters

We see the silly game-birds drop.
We beat the trees and put them up
And fire. A cock falls like a plane
Winged in a war-film, coiling out
Of that undone comparison
To Plato's form and first idea,
Salt of the big screen everywhere.

I have a thorn-stick. In a line
We beaters walk, knock, hoot and call.
Hen-pheasants fly, the twelve-bores crash,
The game fall quickly to the ground
And never rise from that soil's ash.
At home I shot a sparrow. Puff!
It spiralled like an autumn leaf.

Birds, you once accompanied
The soul to heaven; now are stuffed
Goose-gullets yielding peerless food
Or low-flying target for the line
Of beaters marching overdue,
Ourselves to end like swaying corn,
Replenishing the Somme and Marne

And ignorance. Our vision's back
In place down this self-conscious world
Projecting sights to self-fulfil,
As though the aim prepared the crack
At which gore pants and pheasants fall,
Winking their feathers' garnet gold,
And dogs pad through the turnip-field.

One day in unfilmed history
The heron's weird umbrella-stick
Expanded; Lady Poverty
Sang in the meadows, glancing up
At various flight and how the lark
That rode out gravity gave praise
To what we now call emptiness.

Apple Incest (i)

I climbed the apple trees today to touch
The tart, stiff, acid, red-green fruit we've had
In each October of our lives. Our sad
Proud father straddled twenty feet and much
Too riskily raised basins, sacks and such
To pick them in. But when an apple's bad
We throw it now across the lane to thud
Into the churchyard wall, and from the crutch
Where branches split and where the ladder leans
We shake, and hear good apples drop to turf.
That fall of apples, oh so sensuous.
I felt my sister's apples, this thing means
That bark-grazed mossy branch we've spoken of
Was formative, bending the shape of love.

Apple Incest (ii)

in the autumn garden, my sister picked
up an apple, from the grass, where it had
fallen, and I climbed the lichen-covered
tree, felt the biggest red-and-green apples,
at the top, and put them in the fold of my
sweater, while a basket was lifted, by a
rope, and I called down, and put twenty apples
in it, including an unripe one, and we
bit it, and tasted its acid, its green acid,
and we climbed the larger tree, and picked the
red-and-green apples, and felt leaves fall,
and heard apples thud, as the wind tugged, and we
put the apples in crates, on the dishevelled
grass, a darker green, than the unripe apples'
curve, and at the last, a branch of apples broke,
with me astride it, and I fell, with twenty
apples and leaves about me, and I dropped to
the grass, bruised, and my sister laughed,
madly, and gave me, in a darkened sty,
the best, roundest apple of all, which I ate,
till we put the crates, in a shed, by the
apple trees, and later had fruit, apples
and green wine, for supper, and many apples
still lay, on the grass, and the next day, we
gathered them in, we apple pickers, we
pluckers and biters of apples, we shakers,
snatchers, gatherers, expenders of apples.

from *A Certain Marvellous Thing* (1993)

The Irish Sea from St Davids

How often you stare at its face
Half-asleep and knowing it makes you so.
Hypnotized by the quietist to and fro.
Helped by it drawing off restlessness.

Waves as primaeval endless re-writing.
Words slipped in, crossed out, crests toppling over
Without punctuation, a passage of water
Weighing its content; waves quoting, citing.

Some the tentative movements of the blind.
Some sewing, weaving and unravelling.
Some come in tired from a day's travelling.
Some wave to you, are just the mind.

Some hit rock then are vertical spray.
Some are young dolphins dozing.
Some are envelopes opening, some closing.
Some launder, dry, and put themselves away.

Tired now and shivering I watch it all.
There's radioactive junk out there.
To think when we were young it was pure.
Tides don't change much. They rise and fall,

Destined in their sea-sway to continue working.
Dumping is the sea's capacity itself.
Divers scratching around the continental shelf,
Doing their pollution research, are just checking.

Beautiful how sea spreads out its hands and repents.
Botulism, chemicals and raw sewage. Then
By degrees next year another thing. Yet again,
Bent on exposing our newest innocence,

As we love to from time to time,
Almost we must go on challenging this place,
A spinning ball, just to survive us.
And so it will. Our children's home.

Children play on the cliff near the edge.
Could I save one, that fell by going too far?
Clamber the outcrop and haul it back from there?
Careful how you withdraw from the ledge

Of these fantasies and return to staring.
On the left, rocks sloshed by the sea's swell.
On the right, the path to the saint's well.
Out front our new-seen sea, weeping, still caring.

Spelling

Is he still it now? Is Jesus
It now, or has it changed now? Is

Jesus still it now, King of
Jews like and the world now? Is he

King now still like they said, like we
Kids were told, is he king still of

Love now, like when in the bombs and
Later the rationing, is he son of

Man as they said or at least
Many said, or some said? Oh. He's

Not now. That's all over and done
Now, that's it then. Oh, right,

Oh, so it's over now. Oh well, it's
Over and gone now. Too bad then. Oh.

In Mem

8 May, 1990

We cruised at 39,000 feet; over
Water it first seemed, but turned out
Westward Ho (well-named) with its long sea
Wall showing up like a black scar –
When the man beside me turned the page.

"Oh...." I said, rather too suddenly. Three
Obituaries as usual, but *John*
Ormond I had not seen, not known, for
Over a year, or so the fleeting time felt.
Out in the wool-clouds that sun gentled.

I looked across the cumulus, wondering
If we hope truly when thinking humans
Integrate, at death, with all that, or what
Iridium this cryst of stars will bring else.
It was daylight out there; as noon, as heaven.

Elegiac

Seals die sad-eyed, whales writhe, fish found dead.
Species mysteriously disappear. Butterflies
Slip away, elephants and rhinos murdered.
Survivors are vermin and beautiful insects.

The atmosphere punctured like stretched rubber.
The forests wither, the lakes burst into flame.
The fuel that pampers us rainbows the air.
The dune beaches are boxed with hotels.

Yobs mob with their broken bottles, admired.
Yacht havens lilt rather softly on oil.
Yellow white black seethe loudly, too openly.
Years at a time drift, faster and faster.

Lying on the moon are a few footprints
Likely to stay exactly so for ever.
Love is a medium, a territory, an air.
Life shifts sideways, by inches in the mind.

Enormous changes are upon us, friend.
Education, the marvellous chance, was rejected.
Euthanasia an urgent and dangerous option.
Electricity, nature's last breath and pulse.

England

Everything is sucked to the middle.
Each screw is tightened, there is no give.
Elastically are stretched like a drum on
England its roads, for pairs to drive across.

If the noise goes on the people will madden.
If it stops they are bewildered, never find
Intent or objectives. There aren't sweet
Items of garden any more, the air unpronged.

Why are our skins flayed to bursting?
Will the millennium crack all open
With the force of a hatching egg?
We are scared. Why doesn't the news stop?

Never in history was there easement.
Nothing seems calm this week. Yet if every
New generation turned looking for ice
North, there'd be merely travel, merely snow.

Nature

Black people increase in number and
Beauty; yellow people always increased
Before white people; white people are
Bothered now and a little tired.
But let us love one another. For

There are too many of us by far
To make the planet ungentle again.
The method is impossible. We can't.
To flay the moment of penetration and
Travail – oh, oh no. Yet these women

Have had enough. They have borne us.
Have nursed us, housed us, held us,
Hugged us. Surely it is time for dreaming.
Home is the windows we stare from.
Huts were fine for the tall and scaled.

Animals, you are no part of the design.
Ants are, fish for a while longer
And birds so long as there is distance.
All the creation looks at the dry river,
Awaiting the outcome of the unintended.

Elegy for the Accidental Dead

These lines are for you, my dying darling.
Tactless to cry, what have we done?
Desperate to aid you saying "all is well"
Despite what for us you bravely bear.

If poetry means anything at all, language lingering
In the memory as chance of healing help,
It must be attempted. Truth standing trial,
Ingenious as it may seem, as weighed words.

Otherwise what mockery is this awful alphabet,
Obscuring all claim to express exactly
By a mere twenty-six signs the sighs
Bereaved ones emanate now, lovers and survivors.

*

Bow doors fatally open, a wave's whole whale
Borne in and slumped about the car cargo's
Hold from wall to wall. Continental containers
Hurled then rolled dizzily, drew drunken

Egregious water which, greasily fouled, filled and
Edged up to deck restaurants. Café coffee
Jogged and lurched, knives and tables tumbled,
Jagged broken glass. Then electric light left.

Black sucked them down screaming. Creamy
Bleary water swilled, backpacks and anoraks,
Shoes floated in the full hull, their own ocean,
Shaved corpses capsized, food flooded.

Maybe the wreck of this daytrip's detritus
Makes careful and true a right sum; somewhere.

*

Worse when one significant cigarette
Was dropped into that tube's flicked fluff
Years had gathered. No escalator escape,
Yards away was air but plywood and plaster

Incinerated and went white-hot,
Incendiary-like. Took in the ticket-
Hall making steps rubber and melting metal's
Hell-hole. No place to hide; hideous

Panic rushed back down past glamorous absurd ads,
Pain as though instant. Lawyers, lorrydrivers,
Accountants, nurses, kids and temp typists
Accepting here so direfully to die.

God perhaps granted swift suffocation.
God's prudent way: oh, the merciful miracle.

*

Horror gentler when just the wind wanders.
Hurricanes are of nature; purer power.
Nonetheless by such flung foliage
Nineteen died that dreadful night. Flashes flew as

Cables, tree-crashed, draped like knotted knitting.
Cabmen died at the wheel when a crane crumbled.
Doughty elm, ash, fir, birch, beech came
Down and bedrooms saw sky. Oak broke

Horses's necks and crushed ewes. Roofs, rafters and
Houses caved in, a pier's sunk section
Drowning a girl. A toppled church spire spirited
Down dew in the next morning's mourning.

Gracefully a beech, falling hugely, hugged and
Gathered in dying arms its own owner there.

*

Where could iron ever hang in air?
White mist curled silkily over its wavering wing
Flowing into sunset as the nose rose.
Flames then in one engine, port petered out.

Wounded like a gull, the injured engine
Wandered gliding weirdly now, the cockpit's co-pilot
Selected computer readings, the people appalled
Silently begging for decent descent.

Disappearing from radar in its swinging sweep,
Disastrously it fell short at the terminal's tarmac
Avalanching to splinters on a main motorway.
Ambulances abundant for the dead; last lights.

Iteration tells nothing. We fall each earthward
In day and year, from sky the furthest fall.

*

Earthquake and flood, tornado, inferno,
Elements; earth, air, water and fire.
Very gently I must close this weary writing,
Violent at my impertinence, and taxing task.

Train crashes recently here three times.
Titanic shadow, thermonuclear Chernobyl.
A coach plunges in Spain, killing many.
Aberfan with its child wreaths withered.

Who did it, we ask? Who is remotely responsible?
Wondering gets nowhere, nor unreal railing.
Youth copes with loss, remorse remains.
Years gone we are still bearing the difference.

How tactless to try a pompous poem,
Hope to allay conscience by a considered
Icon you stick on a one-off urn.
I can give only a layout of letters.

Ferry them, good Jesus, across the salt Styx.
Fly them to safety in your gone heaven.
Bury them under trees in the green ground.
Bring them from the fire, that their calm come.

Metaphor: *May light perpetual shine upon them.*
Mediaeval minds thus made praise prayer.
New times like ours are new in nervousness.
Now to attempt quiet grief; to say farewell.

| 5.3.1987 | 16.10.1987 | 18.11.1987 | 8.1.1989 |
| Zeebrugge | King's Cross | hurricane | Kegworth |

and the others

In the Box

Father, I have sinned and I confess.
For I am white, male and middle-class and

Was brought up in the south-east of England.
Wretched I turn desperately to you asking what

To do with these appalling errors. I have
Tried living in Canada five years and (oh shame,

Shame) in Wales twenty-five, running a cockney
Stepney youth club, stopping my offspring

(Both male too God forgive me) from yuppie-talk and
Bringing home their ghastly Oxbridge friends, I

Even give a percentage to selected charities.
Every day I deprave myself just the same,

And now know not where to turn. The worst
Aspect is this nauseating guilt-complex which

Makes me ape people's accents, pretend to like
Music-murder on the streets and all the time

Really just avoiding women, patronizing blacks and
Releasing aggro on youth and equals. God, it festers,

Old plants lose their blossoms (OK like men
Other parts, which in my case don't reach I

Guess), they turn brown and a nasty smell and die.
God. God. Did I really think all those Tory things

In those earlier years, and am stuck with them as
If no good feeling, no love, ever moved me? I come to

You for forgiveness, yes, but for guidance too in my
Years left, such as may be granted. The millennium

Comes nearer, the planet's population groups realign
Casually, cautiously and creatively, and old material

Declines as it should and must. Forgive my reactionary
Demeanour; it is a mere stuck groove and a worn

Lazy failure to rotate on the poor axis of flesh.
Life, as always, goes. I've had mine. Forgive, father.

Lucy

The word is light.
Then switched on, "light".

Sunlight is LIGHT.
Stained glass gives LxIeGwHaT.

Hidden light is (light).
Humour is? light?

Jewels sparkle l*i*g*h*t.
Joy flashes: light!

Bowls of fruit are light.
Boy twins are light.

Light on your dear face,
Like that, is sheer grace.

The Way it Looks Right Now

Light shines on everything.
Lazy, lonely light, on bedsteads,
Lines of trees, and verandahs. It
Lends authority to bollards.

Oh but that barely starts it!
Opulence and shit; radios;
Open and shut doors; pyramids,
Otters and rats – the light joins all.

Sunlight that is, not mere grey
Sultry afternoon atmospherics.
Shining entails a beam. Whether on
Sugar-lumps or mountain ranges.

Hence this light we crave can never
Hide a thing. In endless light
Heat, not truth, is what's redundant.
However, as Bacon said, a lie

Is somehow attractive, and we can't
Imagine all bare to the lamps
Incessantly. Many indeed want dark.
It just means that both cherish.

But where do all the people
Belong in this? In sunlight too?
Blacks, child-victims, women,
Buddhists, Iranians, Tibetans and Brits

Traverse the road in jeans and
T-shirt monogram; swear, eat and
Troublemake. We shiver and are
Tormented but light comes again.

And if we love it ourselves, we
Are arraigned and borne out to
An integration: we end there
Answerable, cheerful, small.

Everything joins cheerfully in light.
Each person, object and insect
Enters its trust and no grief lasting.
Even dark laughs aloud at such ending.

The Estuary

It sank into memory, this mud, as
If snow or glass lay on it, or white light

With a weird electron charge
Working, mere search getting you nowhere

On film, or in a book,
Or down there in your earlier mind.

Last week, one stormy day
Late afternoon, late autumn in the sun,

We saw the river's bend
White-hot, pure white below the black

Rain-clouds, making a white
Rare glow, almost as though too hot

To touch. It fused itself
Through every sentence that you spoke,

And bent round like a moon,
A grey horseshoe, a great loud meander

In the daytime. Some new
Injection of cheap housing, too,

Felt its way down the bank too
Fast, to a flyover and underpass

Quite close to what the people felt,
Quietly expecting life, or bearing it.

We didn't find a thing;
What to do, what space-time is or matter

(Truths water, cloud and air are meant
To yield up of their natures),

But no success either
By face-on probe or brainwork alone;

Just that incredible shine,
Jostling the bridge and wharf-piles,

Up from the river sliding by,
Unmoved by any watching; and the people walking

On the esplanade, like handwriting,
Opening their faces to each other, then

Going back to their cars,
Given a new touch from the sky's light.

So: when one tries for "thought" from
Such things, or "life", or "environment",

All just slips from the mind
And vanishes; only when more is dreaded

Does their resting there seem
Double, like a current that eddies backwards

Oddly twisting, even when
On ebb to the barrage below. Anyway,

At last we left, wondering if all that
Appears round here, even pollution, is the same,

Castle now crumbling away,
Cathedral used up, both so old yet both

Like deer silting down to the river,
Licking the water that steered there first,

Arriving never, taking mental/chemical
Advances in their stride, or rejecting them still.

Henry Vaughan Observes from Wherever

I saw eternity the other night
In a great ring of pure and endless light;

London orbital emm twenty-five,
Lilting and twining on its wounded curve

Beatifically shrunk from my dark above.
Below is where persons sleep and live;

Hairdressers, tombs, cheap sex, gardens,
Heathrow for a time in geometry's pylons,

Filtering through the deep terrain's scar.
Field's stamps, quarries, the wet windsurfer.

Clockwise and anti-clockwise spins my clock,
Counting down the century's end on tarmac.

Up There on His Horse

The holly with its brilliant berries of blood.
The footprint lying in the centuries' snow.

Des Dolan sits up there on his horse
Downing punch at the Boxing Day meet in the morning.

He is Master of the Hounds in his red coat.
Hegel looked up at Napoleon once

Like that, numbed at the arsenal of power
Locked on one saddle, out in the agora.

Once he nearly played rugby for Ireland.
Only the selectors determined otherwise.

Ants suffer, and mice do, and petrels, and fish.
And all God's creatures in their kind.

A Swarm of Bees

Random flying bees shot round
Their nucleus like electrons wound
In orbits on an atom's mind.

The population of a town.
A punchball hanging upside down.
A huge ripe pear, a buzzing one.

They crawled, as on each other's mat,
Or like on some tweed overcoat
Where stitching's come alive, not flat.

An expert came and tip-toed up
To shake the curved branch to the top
Neatly and make the whole swarm drop

Like a gold studded brooch in air,
Into a grocer's carton where
As with a splash to disappear

Completely, though there still were some
Delayers, bees that dribbled from
The box's side like liquid, gum.

The bees flew quietly round and round.
At midnight, TV changed the sound.
By satellite the camera panned

Up from the U.S. Superbowl,
Up, up through the night until
The stadium was a swarm of small

And helmeted men, gold at midnight,
The opponent team in blazing white
Like light, like intellectual light

That Dante saw, too bright to see.
Still from our loaded apple tree
Pure gold dripped from the honey bee.

The A40 Wolvercote Roundabout at Oxford

"O" the ubiquitous, the wheel.
A while if only for a while.
A lawn reflecting orange light.
A helipad whence to depart.

Why is he restless? Moons about?
Disturbs the static April night?
O the ubiquitous prayer-wheel,
The ring of lamp-posts tapering tall.

"Welcome to Scholars' Oxenford"
And watch the town roulette-wheel speed
Its bits of centrifugal thought
Off at all angles to the night

As cars brake to its edge, then yield
To let a prior group roar ahead
Then move themselves, or tucked behind
Swing to an exit out beyond,

An arc of concentrated thought.
He paced a little, sensed them do it,
Sat on a civic bench to watch
Them merge and hesitate, guess which

Split-second move a car would make
So miss some other overtake
Some other. None of them remained
More than an instant in his mind,

Not knowing what each driver bore
Most deeply, fears, obsessions, for
Those shed, like clothes, they dropped away
For one lone vagrant passer-by

Witnessing all their stop-start game.
He only saw them go and come
Lane-dodging, weaving, and the wheel
Their curvings made contain them all

As persons, work to suck them in
To this spun centre with its own
Illuminata, then away
To "Stratford, The North", infinity

Lingua Duplex

And she is gone.
His sedge anon,
Heeds in a song,
And she is gone.

Age end his son.
Side on he sang,
One has signed
And she is gone.

One snag I shed
Oh, gains, needs,
God has seen in
And she is gone.

Seasoned nigh,
Send a one sigh,
O ensign shade,
And she is gone.

Seeding on ash
Digs he as none?
Sand he goes in
And she is gone.

A tortured man,
Oh that I am,
Bent in a name.
Nowhere was home.

A tortured man,
O that I am,
A tot, a him,
Bent in a name.

Bent in a name.
A tin man been.
How we see no harm.
Nowhere was home.

He worse he woman
Nine-beat man
Mandate or rut.
O that I am.

*

1) his stormy herd helped: that sin won all

2) deer awaken to morning; his the mute sleep:
 wealth is idle, see the deaths tremble

3) or myths rouse Lethe. these emotions heal darkness,
 pet rage, the hashish menu is off;

4) the lark died halfway to heaven; Eve hollow girl,
 at the fight oh how you fail us;
 watch my deft foot, the sound of rhythm, fair to the martyr;

5) riper than a tree fount in blossom, ephebe, free enemies
 met peace:
 who, hip autumn city? the day returns, the moon in love;

6) dodge eye, fly home, world's lonely music falls,
 harmony's last leaf;
 old field shire fell, and nowhere without lover.

(Psalm xxiii)

*

That you will note was an anagram.
The same letters in different positions.
Of course, the second always sounds awkward.
Lucky overcrowding is less fuss.

Tall amateur wants, oh, no way gain.
Finesse tenses, meteors, half-pint editors.
As we who understand, cool red sky was a focus
Cooks scurry, slugs sin, few lived.

*

Good poetry today is vernacular.
bleeding shit fuckin cunt bleedin ell
He anagrammed it nine times at Paddington.
Louder and louder.
Louder, louder and louder.

British Rail Paddington
air bird sand point light

William Shakespeare
seek a wall, praise him

those twenty-six letters
text, show, interest, style

true mind's rudiments
ABC is basic

certainly neat lyric
chiasmus has music

*

Lake District
trick details

Welsh Tourist Board
showed tribal routs

Oxford and Cambridge
add red BA from coxing

there is no woodland
one oh, world instead

sectional coastline
or men invent environment

nostalgia lost again
another on earth

a theology of people and the planet
elephant, pony, pelt, hoof, toad, eagle

turns same thoughts present
greatness thrust upon them

Terry Waite
a writer yet

Mother Teresa
O rarest theme

*

Government loyalty undermined from the start
Government loyalty underlined from the start

Not particularly the dates
Note particularly the dates

The homeless want to buy a house
The homeless went to buy a house

They will punish cruelty without compassion
They will punish cruelly without compassion

Race appears to race to forbear
Race appeals to race to forbear

*

All must be seen,
  Tell, see as numb,

Pysche outward
  Cheaty words up

Telegraph, Times
  Their pages melt

The stitching shows
  Which ghost isn't set;

Toilets and shit
  Last on this tide

Black yellow white red
  It wrecked hello by law

Become rage not walk,
  We cram a token globe,

Nimby crank today,
  Not in my back yard.

By far we are too many
  We are too many by far

*

O friend stop moaning!
In ode of past morning

Why this, how can I sing?
I own his shy watching

Observe, pleb peacemonger
Bare people becoming verse

Her ire urges deterrent sense
Greener trees end their users

History sweeps wrath, fan told.
For the windows play the stars

*

split ghost, her engulf it all, wept on reprisal,
sink prose, a rook could, rose flux Gaia,
able champ, begin Chester, sits in hunger,
education's far ray, earls, to its perch,
car fuse bio-warn, filled hot growth,
hang steel, incandescent hill sigh zigzag north

spotlights, in the full glare, ripples on water,
pink roses, Kodacolour, four galaxies,
Palm beach, the big screen, the rising sun,
your radiant faces, laser, the tropics,
surface, rainbow, light of the world,
the angels, ah, intense scorching dazzling light

for then lamps create
the last performance

fuel vice, join strength
the curving jet flies on

plainly to use
easy to pun ill

a gender enraged
 seek a man's namesakes

noon miners blend but wilt
 buried not ten miles below

enter at last the poor and needy
 rest not the dear planet, one day

from *Genesis* (1996)

Genesis

the evening the
the morning the

trees
      fishes

and God said

and
      the fifth day

light on the waters

      man

the evening the
the morning the

Science Fiction

Dinosaurs first, aeons before our time.
Does it go always from big to small?
Deer, elephants and whales met their
Demise next, then lions and bears.

Smaller creatures disappeared
Supplying quotas of meat. Others
Simply ceased procreation. Wolves
Surrendered way back to the cold.

Foxes were drubbed out of life by
Farmers not without brief resistance.
Ferrets assisted with smaller prey
Flushing out their lairs. Then they

Went too followed by marmots and
Water rats. Salmon got hooked on
Water shortage or its pollution.
Weasels escaped into wire netting.

Toads were levelled by every kind of
Tyre that we invented. Hoopoes flew up
To the sky then glided down finding on
Tarmac no more slugs or worms. For

Ants also vanished now, some time
After the chafer's exit. Bees went mental
And killed their queens. Smaller termites
Ate each other, lacking flesh to feed on.

Briefly humans had casualties too, yet
Bearing in mind our expansion to many
Billions it meant little. All died out
Bar humans, we survived. All but humans gone.

Left so, research dwelt on physioneural
Life-support where nutrition is concept
Like mathematics. It was so calm at
Last. Other factors, even fear, diminished.

No problem, no "upset balance of
Nature". All was most gently ordered.
New-age man hence strode forward into
Notions of being hitherto unimagined.

Marathon

In rain, two hundred runners streaming
Past us yet so out of reach
It felt they or ourselves were dreaming.
Stirred, we drove ahead to watch
And parked. The hazels dripped. A man
Tore by at murderous cold speed,
Dead silent, pounding on the road.

Second and third ran powerfully.
Groups next with oddly awkward gait,
Their minds obsessed with healthful flight.
Then masses, bunched and talkative
As amateurs, at play for love.
Then stragglers in threes and twos
And ones, mud splashing round their toes.

Later, through wheat, the thin white line
Far off, slow prisoners in a chain.
Earth's low flameless fire, their motion
Rhythmic as a crescent ocean.
In from the wet they took their showers,
Towelled, dressed, then out for home rejoined
Long marathons of crawling cars.

The Fifth Suit

My grandfather had these five three-piece suits.
I never saw him in any other thing.
The best was for annual dinner or wedding.
The second was 'best', Sundays and special nights.
His tailor cut them exactly out for him
From a striped grey, deep blue, and then some.

The third one the old man wore every day
In his working week. It was just as good
As the fourth, and when at the bus-stop he stood
In the queue he looked distinguished the way
Accountants used to. He wore a bowler hat.
On his office door was a small brass plate.

You'll have guessed the fourth was his change
For the evenings, and the fifth for gardening.
Foot on a spade, correctly attired, digging
With his jacket taken off now – he would arrange
It first on the back gate like a scarecrow.
But the one thing we always never knew

Was the dreaded doom of the fifth suit every year.
For, once a year, he was fitted for a new one.
And all the five suits were relegated down
A slot – wedding to Sunday, Sunday to daily wear.
The fourth, at least still alive, went to the shed.
But the fifth, by God I shrank, for that suit was dead

And *never seen again*. We never saw it leave.
Cast into outer darkness, whirling and flailing
Its legs and sleeves, to the Milky Way in wailing
And gnashing of teeth, no fifth suit did ever survive.
Grandpa was chapel. I was haunted, I know.
Probably it went to Oxfam, or that scarecrow.

Attempt

true story, Bosnia, 1993

This acquaintance had driven
To that land with supplies but
The resident murderers
Took away her driver

Whose head they sheared off
Whole at the dripping neck
Whereupon they kicked it
Whooping and playing football.

Once a holy man said we
Only ever suffer such
Onus as we are capable
Of bearing; this could be true.

Humour also played its part.
His amputated thing they
Held up like a grenade,
Hooraying the while.

Next month she went again,
Never one to back off from
New challenges or suchlike
Neurotic forebodings.

I must predict (she said)
I won't return this time.
Intuition mutters
It's inconceivable, this time.

She was so nearly right.
Shelled from a low hill her
Small van was hurled
Sixty yards with her in it.

Mission over. And yet
Meanwhile each day since,
More volunteers have gone in; as
Misguided, as foolish, as blind,

Carrying their boxes of
Comfort in these strange
Convoys of faint faith,
Clear on no destination bar

Action alone, as though to
Attempt such salvation
Aims at value itself.
At least get that through.

In the Country

to be alone now is
to be as a child
told parents were dead. it is
to see a seat with no one

sitting there, a field
scene with no person,
sunset with no witness.
seaside and the swimmers gone.

home is here, one's
house is warm, indeed
hearth and rug dispense
heat from the coal's

black solid. there are
books as before, one's
bedroom as before, to
be silent is now rare

proportion. currants and
plums give way to
passion-fruit, greenhouses are
plastic, weather-resistant

and grey. there's no
answer to such and none to
ask, the landscape's
arsenal of cars is

our voice and sole enouncement.
only the self propounds,
otherness is one's world
of orbit as of existence.

*

never despair friend
no place derelict utterly,
nothing fully bereft.
now is the noon, the moment

for galactic blazes beginning,
fire burst and crackle,
fancies and fantasies,
flash, sparkle and flare

extended media-wise.
earth and ecstasy,
Eve her very self and
Eden too at last full-lettered.

aa bb cc dd ee ff gg
hh ii jj kk ll light
light light light light
light light light light

light li*ht light light
ligt light light light
lightXlight*light light
light light light light

light light light light
light light light light
light*light light light
light light light light

light light light light
light light*light light
lightS*light l**ight light
light light light light

iqzan blewo pcurj qvxde
fhkms tyaep dnxow htivm
rguyf bcjik lqzsu*xrzjc
alvpm bnoxy dfgqt hkesw

light light light light
light light light light
light*light light light
light light light light

mmmmm mmmmm
mmmmm mmmmm
mmmmm mmmmm
mmmmm mmmmm

nnnnn nnnnn nnnnn nnnnn
ngngng ngngng ngngng ngngng
ooooo ooooo ooooo ooooo
ooooo ooooo ooooo ooooo

pqr s t u v w x y z
opq r s t u v w x y
nop q r s t u v w x
mno p q r s t u v w

pqr s t u v w x y z
opq r s t u v w x y
no p q r s t u v w x
mno p q r s t u v w

*

by the trees the twilight
begins rotation's work. night's
branches grey over, the hills'
bulge frightens them no more as

when everyone was here
with us but also each other.
where they are is no
wonder; now trees and soil come

in each year of our best
inception. younger and not sad
I know these magpies and grass
instinct with friendship and love.

That Tree is Blue

That tree is moonlit blue, she said quickly.
But that is what I saw too he replied,
Nothing but that: the moon hanging low
With nothing but that cheetah-bird, bare
And with nothing but. That forked branch
Broken and with nothing but that a few black
Leaves broken and with nothing but that promise
She leaves broken and with nothing but that
Love she leaves. Broken and with nothing but
That *love she leaves, broken and with nothing*
But that *love she leaves, broken and with*
Nothing but that *love she leaves, broken and*
With nothing but that tree of love which is
Blue quickly, she said and oh I saw he replied.

October

C.C. d 14 October 1993
M.W. d 25 October 1993
P.V. d 29 October 1993

The details here are
True, as is the autumn
Time October: it was as I
Tell it: what I'm saying is true.

Again exploiting how our
Alphabet spreads and scatters,
Asking it to be the bits
And pieces, the twigs and leaves.

Both of us stunned but way
Beyond blaming anything; to
Be candid it's work to
Begin on 'green' or much else.

*

When the phone rang first
We were picking at cheese and grapes.
What is happening (defensively
We asked) to these decades?

Friends; close neighbours and
Farmers; his wife so inward
Flung herself that last morning
From the new bridge's girders

Into the airslip. It stands at
Immense height, the black water
Icy even for mid-October,
Ink near frozen. The city

Shone enchanted like her
Streaming hair and the bent
Smile of curiosity and calm
She always had, no more.

All of us falling into her
Abyss followed her, the very
Atmosphere there gyrated,
Attitudes spun, plans dipped.

*

When it rang the second time
We were here far west and secluded.
Woods with their trees all
Wonderful orange red and brown.

His voice high-pitched and thin.
His son in Auckland who driving
Had stopped to mend a tyre was
Hacked down by a van on a country

Road at night. The boy's friends
Reached him in seconds. None
Recalled even a spasm. At least
Relief there was no pain, yet perhaps

Vainly we wondered if soft
Views might assuage, the cottage rest.
Various therapies; them maybe
Visit out here, regather here.

Groping from the car all three made
Grief's very image, in our rooms
Gave vent and clung then calmed.
Grass and low dunes held us,

Seashore the levels that we walked,
Sanding our feet as in the old days.
Sinking clouds failed twilight till
Sorrow fell and we drove them back.

Now flown home his ashes are interred
Next to a fellow-student dead
Newly of cancer. The stone church
Nestled by the cliff in trees: it did.

*

A third time that phone, exactly
As we entered the door: that
Actual minute: shock grips, more
Acute never happened, couldn't be.

Just for the record: debt already
Jumping him he uninsured (still no
Job) then "was in collision with" a cream
Jaguar so later chose his way out.

Mindful a second (suicide too) as
Marx said is farce I add no
More here, the grievous
Moment enough for her scars.

*

Loved, dear, so close, so known.
Losses like this sear one, rinse, leave us
Limp and arbitrary survivors,
Lacking a plan: our projects' phases,

Rain-forest obliteration,
Research on the two-week embryo,
Radiation as cause of leukemia,
Ravaging tourist migrations –

It hangs right aside, such
Individual grief, from these ecological
Imperatives; they are the public tally
In figures of pain come home.

My letter-work too subsides (friends call it
Mania); fine as formal, suddenly it
Makes no sense from the heart,
Means nothing in silence. How do

You say what you feel, if all is internal?
You don't feel so much years older as
Years deeper. This realising, that
Yesterday they were alive but not today,

Crushes serenity. It is itself that
Car-crash we daily dread and live in
Constant terror of. It crumbles us.
Concisely, curtly, a torch is put out.

Everyone there who shoulders such
Extremity of grief – who also could
Eventually be struck down some such
Evening as, it chances, I write –

Helplessly watch, as theories evaporate,
Hoped proposals dangle, dear friends' days
Hollow out like their eyes for years ahead.
How we lack old wisdom a new way.

*

116

We can't unknow what has been found.
Worlds stud the night sky like dots or
Wheel almost invisibly slowly in
Wastes of tumescent space. There

Is no endless earth or ploughed
Infinite vegetation. No roots deep
In flat bottomless soil. The world
Is stressed like a bridge. Man's

Usual ancient sense of solid earth
Under our soles as our home's
Ultimate expression, is no more. How
Utter is one's love for these unpublic

Persons and single casualties.
Please planet please, save us; be
Placated by our late desperation.
Pardon our fateful expanse, our expense.

After Simone Weil

at Gloucester

Suffering's no problem.
Simply bereaved or jobless.
Sanity floats alongside.

Affliction, though, is hell.
Accompanied by pain but also
Acutely numbed in its nature.

It is the sump of degradation.
It genders distaste and disgust.
It leaves you a half-crushed worm.

Christ himself was afflicted.
Crime and sin the excuse.
Compassion is impossible.

They don't want it even themselves.
They are condemned, condemned.
They stain us with their poisoned light.

Fathomless void, the afflicted are
Frozen to the soul so deep they
Feel never person again.

Brought there right from the start
By fact and matter's very
Being. Genes: some bastard: war.

Why this unspeakable blackness?
What Simone wrote on the subject
Weaves notions still barely credible.

Love being no dimension
Locates love no matter how far. Its
Lack no matter how near.

118

Therefore an infinite love
Treads infinity from God to God.
That's an awful lot of space;

No wonder atheists believe
Nothing else exists.
Nothing does, not materially.

On the other hand there's
Obedience. Of waves wrecking ships.
Of autumn leaves. Of sunlight.

This river's ripples, for instance.
The railway slices and glints.
Typists and roadmen eat snacks,

Absorb fast-food by the cathedral
And continue. Sun warms, it soaks.
"All the world down here is beautiful."

Why the hell? Because choiceless.
Will needs will, said Nietzsche.
Won't work on coal. Can't kick the rock.

Yet the afflicted do see God?
You could say that, she tells us.
Yesterday's dream their dark star.

Time I went home. The car-parking
Ticket's expired. Love, pain,
Terror, light and evil. That's all.

The Annual Fair

What is a blind man's look?
  Is he thinking?

Maybe there's some kind of inward book.
  Maybe he's sinking

In a darkness several feet under
  With no window,

His friend an extrovert pink albino
  Hair white as snow;

Another girl's eyes sunk in the pits
  Of their sockets, wits

Gob-smacked. Eyeballs rolled up
  Into the skull's top,

One eye stares, the other shut;
  Some smile, some not;

All beavering away at their projects.
  Gadgets:

Blind Scrabble set, blind chess,
  Edged trays for no mess,

Sensitized radio controls (not TV),
  White stick wired electronically;

And they make outstanding piano-tuners
  We're told; masseurs, crooners

Even, or this one was, articulating
  Her thing

At this Blind College's Annual Fair,
   Guide dogs everywhere.

It is a perfect scene
   (For us, I mean),

The mellow building with its gables,
   The bright green lawns and salad tables.

Tea-time

A blood-red teapot, apple-shaped, too plain
Beside a blue jug, urn-squared, cobalt blue.
A plate with double-blue lines and a stain

Around a circular track, blue nuts, a few
Leaves hung in navy blue (reflecting red
From the light's teapot) and the day a view

Of blue sea and a pink-red sunset shed
On a willow-pattern saucer and its cup,
A Chinese fence with strawberries abed,

By cherry trees and kingfishers flung up
At azure sky. Pagoda with my spoon
Across it like a humped bridge; girls; a pup;

A butterfly and tea. The afternoon
With cut bread spread with jam and raspberry,
Of flaking red and glass; we outstare alone

The peacock's world. A miniature tea-world.
Five billion times are you and me arranged.
Left motionless on china. If we could

All stay so, unpolluted, nothing changed.

Elegy for the Plank Man

A man aged 66 was shot dead yesterday as he tried to stop a raid on
security guards by attacking the robbers with two planks of wood. Mr
Donald Kell, a pensioner, lived with his wife in a council flat 200 yards
away in Finchley, North London.

As the robbers fled with £500 to a getaway car the father-of-two lay
dying on the pavement murmuring: "What have they done to me?" He
had been on his way to put up two 30in shelves for a neighbour.

Commander John O'Connor, head of the Scotland Yard Flying Squad,
said "The man was astonishingly brave. We will move heaven and earth
to find these people."

From The Times, *27 July, 1989*

Our earth spun like a dog shaking spume
Off its fur, rain-forests caught fire for
Millions of pesos to arable and ash.
Maybe I've forgotten motorways maturing

For the first time. He was sixty-six.
Front-page news dying, a laughable leaf
Askew on the pavement, shot in his shorts and
Anonymous all life and then fame's fate.

Photo was a home-camera blow-up, he can't
Pose now. He smiles at disturbing distance,
Through frosted glass almost, a being beyond
Time in the blurred newsprint journalists enjoy.

Lugging his planks he reached Golders Green
Lloyds Bank. Two thugs "in their '30s or '40s,
Stockily built, unmasked and with beer bellies"
Suddenly rushed the security guards. Goodness,

If it exists, is very tiny, invisible even
It seems, a germ ill-advised and both those
Robbers sensed its flash when he just jumped
Right in with his plank. On his own, and said one

Mr Patel (who gave chase): "He just came and came,
Madly, with his plank." They punched and pushed
Him, kicked him to the ground but he returned,
Hoisting his plank like a triumphant tree

From which came shelves for a near neighbour.
For he helped people, his wife whispered.
A woman laid a blanket on the plank man
As he died murmuring, "What have they done to me?"

Christ too with two timbers staggered and ended
Crucified, a robber each side. Curious coincidence,
That, chance no doubt but what wood I wonder
Twirled green for the plank man. For Finchley

Sweltered leafily that day. In hot hatless
Summer, lime avenues budding when a body
Reddened like a poppy, global greenhouses
Reversed a moment as businessmen, buses,

Pizza-Hut and Boots flared their foliage
Prior to exodus, the awakening weekend.
Couples on tour in England's last landscape
Cuddled in the grass, Gloucestershire grew

Lusher and Devon dreamed butterflies and bees.
Lakeland admired as everyone left London
Exhausted, roads clogged with tourism's traffic.
England slumped. "What have you done to me, man?"

The Wye below Bredwardine

The banks are steep. Drought. Water too low.
Too many trees by it too, it feels. Yet
They impress heavily, this hot calm day.
Trees hang and bulge over, and peer right down.
Thirsty alders lean over, the bane of water.

Huge plate-glass windows sliding along
Horizontally, slowly rotate as they go. No
Hurry in such drift. And when flies and seeds
Hit it, dartboards widen and meet the dead
Hauteur of the banks, their raw nettle clumps.

Lower down these panes bump submerged reefs,
Lazily give, yet resist quite breaking.
Little folds and pleats adjust the Wye's surface.
Leaning over you see its tiny corkscrewings,
Like pocks on estuary mud, but down water.

Suddenly, near one bank in a patch of weedy
Sunlight, a blue shoal of chub. And,
Several feet down by the bridge's piles, one
Salmon flickered deep like a neon light.
Swinging on a branch, a tyre half-submerged.

What ease has this tonnage of sedately moving
Water. Sleepily it stirs, then enfolded
With so slight a turn rolls over in bed and
Weighs sideways down again. A hundred metres
Wide. Leaves, bubbles, downy stuff, flies.

It is evening sunlight. Already. Lambs baa.
I love you, sylvan Wye, or would do so
If that were tenable, correct, and still allowed.
Instead, I say too many trees. Traherne himself
Imagined this heaven. Is there hope? Swans arrive.

Wind Machines near Bridgend

Huge kisses on stalks. Kinder.
Skyline. Skyline. Skyline. Skyline.
Foxgloves. Blooms. smoolB. sevolgxoF.
Arms akimbo, semaphore. All-Stars.

Skyline. Skyline. Skyline. Skyline.
Angels, *aggeloi*, messengers from God.
New-born children. Axe to the root.
Larks rise, the spacemen have landed.

Tossing their heads in sprightly dance.
X is the spot. Bare range exchanges.
A thick hum emits from there all day
To those who go near or live so near.

They have come from a far country.
Etch not our awkward dialects.
Air is their food, their home is air.
Fluttering and dancing in the breeze.

Boxes. Ekko. Distaffs. Cool.
Crucify now and dance to the tree.
Hills asleep and under not asunder.
Am tallness to the tall blue blue.

So Far

apples are computers

beaches are creches

cars are loud-hailers

days are entitlement

earth is afternoons

fuel is decorum

grass is chrome yellow

hills are athletics

industry is sculpture

jeans are photography

kinship is unlikely

law is new physics

murder is abandon

neon is moonlight

offices are funtime

people are exceptions

quiet is recalled

rivers are fibreglass

sky is orchestral

tarmac is helium

understanding is microdot

victims are neighbours

water is consumption

x is all over

youth is authority

zeal is the extent

from *Late Thoughts in March* (1999)

Coda

Always, the leaf-driving
wind and lashing rain to rattle
doors and bring branches, twigs to drop
on roads to snap there and be raddled equally
and the silence of this house, my wrists'
movement audible as I write, and my
thoughts so too.

A sidelong moon has grey cloud flung
across it like lace curtain for a
watcher outside, a path's flat
slabs wet-shining to a cottage door, with
dark panes besides, as from the drawing of
a child, and the child inside, cold white
hands round a teacup, remembering, alone.

There were two sheepdogs as I walked
in the hail and under the lane's electric
light, but one is missing now, I call and
call but still he does not come, the
other's tousled wispy hair, slinks with
me as a car passes, with sugary
whiff of gasoline.

Back in the house, fists on chin and
thought, thought, thought. The moon
cracked autumn branches centuries ago;
it will again; the village's lights
flick on at tea-time one by one and falling
leaves handwrite across the grass;
we will not change, we will not change

Rain

Great walls of mist moved inland
From estuary to woods, cupfuls of water
Cataracted from the drain-pipe, spewed
On the lawn and the dog's
Wet coat gripping him, hung snarling
To him till he shivered and slunk off.
The turned earth seeped, the radio's
Classical music trilled alongside
The wind's storm. A man was alone,
Was ready to write and he wrote, lurching
On sound not footprints as one might through snow.

He sat at a table as on a moor,
His elbows two rocks. Thinking
Was thanking that amalgam of ruined wind,
Of winter leaves like paint-brushes or dead
Crows in trees; of flapped, flicked rain.
The black-and-white dog was now a dot.
To think had always been bedlam,
Images too fast for facts' contingencies,
Like tools oiled carefully in a shed, that he
Might use, or they use him; to feel
The last green year there, the branches
And cumulus of the sky, but that seasons
Too caused gale in their four orders.

The First Severn Bridge

Up to its paying turnpike, towed
In cars like beetles veering the road.
Across the huge arc tensed and bowed,
We tourist drivers glance up, awed.

Enormous bobbins taper down.
Cables bear their stanchions' strain.
Trusses grip their block's foundation.
Rockers stress all loads to one.

The flat crown is a liner's deck.
Thunk, and a vast container truck
Slots in behind the next car back.
Far out the holm sleeps in its rock.

Hell, bridge, does any one of us
Not feel non-being under us?
What sort of being hung like this?
Constructed to outstare our gaze.

A Third Place

Its crackling unsubtle hugeness under snow
And like for some panoramic camera that pink glow
Redeemed are for me the underpinning thought
And first colour. I've been years away now

From that packed, spaced-out and all-season ranch.
Indian, Saxon, Eskimo and French
Were its forced peoples, and the one thin red-hot
Railroad has pushed and carved as though for every inch

Of track by dynamite-blasting excavation.
That route bought its figure-of-eight elevation
From the mountain ranges with such locomotive sweat
Of gross energy as to attempt a single nation

Thought geographically impossible. To me
It has all deepened and unified merely
To the irreducibly perceived; what cannot
Now be other than past, unshiftable reality.

A lifetime back I did live there. I see towns of maples
Lilting in tuneful avenues, and clap-board steeples
On pioneer churches and transcontinental freight
Shunting through the snow on greens, purples

And whites of mountain-sides. Naturally it seemed
An incomplete culture then, that what many deemed
Generations earlier an uncertain thing,
Must still stay out there beyond reach in such untamed

Lake-pocked forest and silent low-slung prairie,
Plain and distance. And the sky, past wiry
Telegraph-cables over littered ghost-town streets,
Simply underlined my own incomplete mind and pure
                                        memory.

In one summer for instance we built a cabin by
Our cottage, in the spruce trees and firs as high
As Canada-geese, us smacking nails into
Knotted timber that smelt of soap and felt as dry

As snuff. The sun on us swung brilliantly between
Clefts of sticky and spiky black branches seen,
As if magnified, through a lens to ignite pulp but
To warm chipmunk and squirrel as well, balm the
                                                    evergreen.

In one fall we drove for days among yellow leaves
And blood-red ones, and had near shaves
Just missing trucks at *No U-Turn* signs. Girls perched
On our knees, we swam in their one-season loves.

In one winter I bought a hockey-stick
And on collapsing ankles had thrills sending the puck
Frictionless down plains and terrains of ice
Like travelling, scored some goals (by luck)

Then licked all my bleeding knuckles. I took
A college course and in vacations work
In a spatter of jobs; department store
Assistant, lifeguard, railway-diner cook

And then reception-clerk at the lush Lake Louise
Hotel, where to a dark lawn lay that turquoise
Stretch of sheer water under a sky all ink-bottle blue.
Such memories. Such splinters of broken-glass memories

From a baggy, shapeless land, that strip
Of rock then snow then town then pine then trap,
Set by trappers in the bush for moose, fox and deer.
That jagged territory pegged out like a map

Seems now mere selectivity and randomness.
And there is, too, the present need to reduce
All I wondered and felt, all my ideology,
To the rawest of mineral, wood, and furs,

Which the indigenous were making then in the new way.
Rising conceptions, techniques and arts to array
And renew their essence as they now proliferate
Just on three thousand miles and currents away.

For I'll never live there again now. They're gone times.
But to recall, by night or day, such stirring names –
Great Bear Lake, Yellowknife, Fort Resolution –
It races the pulse, brings back a couple of dreams.

Follow the Foliage

for Morris and Sue Schopf

An American philosopher
Wrote under trees, so it is said
In this encyclopaedia.
Mauve, yellow, burnt sienna, red,
The autumn leaves fell round his head
Like fancies chasing round his head.
It was Thoreau. One day this man

Read how the Buddha picked some leaves,
And showed his followers and said
"The forest's foliage, next to these,
Is all the thoughts I could have said.
Those were just some." Last year in Maine
All my New England colleagues said
Follow the foliage. So we did.

Next year we followed it again.
Hourly reports on radio
Broadcast the turning leaves. A day
Can set the maple trees on fire
In orange tongues, and from your car
You kind of see the waves recede
Like daylight full of clouds at speed

In wave on wave, a week or more
Chasing them up to Canada.
The birch leaf goes a rustier red.
The tulip leaf is like a spade.
I guess I'm no philosopher.
We saw a million leaves last fall
And no thought bothered us at all.

Gatwick: Planes Landing and Leaving

Dots shine, they twinkle in the sun.
Then swell, descending from the clouds,
A queue of dots, then land their shrouds
As though to skate the world is fun.
They come and come, out of the sun.

They track and taxi into place
Then charge, a sudden lurch of speed
Before their lift-offs into space.
Each a huge double-decker bus.
At every window-slot, a face.

An Abortion

And he went to the inn, and out to
the building at the back, the decrepit stable,
and he had to know, if they were there, in the
quiet lofts, the cattle stalls, whether it
was true, and precisely what was true, and he
entered, to the glimmer of light, and the
noise of the inn, was nearby, yet he excluded it
completely, shut it out, and saw a small
shawled woman, and a thin man, an indecisive
one, and others with them, sheep tenders,
bearded, who were uncertain, unsettled and
afraid, he thought, and it was dark though,
cobwebby, despite the oxen's oaty breath,
a moth-eaten donkey, a camel, and a candle,
and a wooden trough, with straw in it, and they
all near it, and he, standing in dung, edging
forward, searching for it, saw it; a minute
foetus, a tiny white thing, not five inches
long, it had been untimely born, and he stared
and stared, and suddenly saw; it was alive,
it was not dead at all, it was its exquisite,
unimaginable and incredible self; and he,
quickened and amazed, ran out to the club, the
pub and the farmer's house, telling everyone there.

Hallucination

Two boys playing on the lawn.
A modest lake left by the rain
Adorns the path beside the lane.
Upside-down the tree-trunks sink
Reflections for a staring man
To see himself in, flooded. Then,
Out from this deep hallucination,
Silent on the cottage lawn
In front of where we used to live,
I see a tiny girl in pink.

Who is she? I know who she is.
The daughter that I never had.
I had two brothers and their dad
Was just an only, like his wife.
A kind of thin, one-gendered life.
My own wife's only sister died.
Two brothers ever at my side,
No girl. Ah, how I wondered who
She was or any like her was.
I stare down at the looking-glass.

For Their Own Good

Dad, do I have to go away?
You'll feel OK in the morning I lied,

Drying his eyes with a baby boy's
Yukkie flannel. So long ago and

Distantly I see those cottage beds
Years back and how each night each

Day piled up to the time being
Young would fade. This final week,

Drunk with prizes, Old Boys and cricket,
Yesterday half-flickers back like some

Damp poster stuck to a wall,
Yellowing the paper. *Parties and*

Decisions and stuff Dad...work and New
York.... don't fret... back in October...

Do you have to go away? All I can say.
Yawns of discernment. Optional now.

Dunblane

We need our children to remain children.
These few will do that for us.

When we die they will still live.
The small bright faces on the sideboard.

Why is our earth out of joint?
There is an answer but not here.

Weeping just audible, near silent.
Threat, torment, fear have the tongue.

Women bear, and then they bear.
To die at four being not thinkable.

Waifs, petals, feathers.
Tiny things, intercede for us.

Nativity

Would you like my breast, she said.
No more than the rest, he said.

Will there be no speech, she said.
Once into the breach, he said.

Shall we have a babe, she said.
Tested in the tube, he said.

Will the sun explode, she said.
If we overload, he said.

I'm your equal now, she said.
Here's the sequel now, he said.

Watering the plants, she said.
Future at a glance, he said.

She: I am essential earth.
He: I follow in your path.

A Later Poet (Maybe Tu Fu)
Reads the Quiet One

The words of Wang Wei:
From his example I
 Endeavour order

First I place my lady
Then her children surely
 As they teach

Procrastination rife
Essential to the cultured life
 I learn such

Smiling, curious
Then look to my house
 Its clapperboards

Flawless in motive
Flush in work and love
 Obdurate

My folk will I bury
Gifted and decently
 At the time

Against ill-luck to come
With order their own
 And their own music

Later Uncollected and New Poems

The 24-Hour-a-day Supermarket in the Countryside

It looked, a little, like a church.
Cut the sentiment, that was no church.

And yet it had a cupola.
Wide entrance and a central tower.

People pushed trolleys through the glass
Into the human night, the air

Is everyone who lives round there.
Where food is night. The blaze of light

Round the refilling area, the pumps
Where cars, refilled, leave for the night,

Their boots well stuffed with food. The smell
Of cultivated hay drifts in

Over the hedges. That's what they called
The place of food; some way to be.

*

They had this animal, it bit and gnawed,
It climbed their ribs inside of them
Like a strenuous ropey gymnast
Training for elusive gold,
That mirage podium of gold.
It scratched, attacked, it howled and gored,
Like nothing their experience
Recalled from previous Januaries,
Junes or Octobers. To tether it, to some degree,
They named it, late one Wednesday night: *Hunger*.
And an unclothed child with pencil limbs
Circled us twice, and dialled a tone: then died.

*

The glass doors clicked against the breeze.
The car park danced, the checkouts sang,
Plump angers ripened on the trees
For picking. Wealth and starvation rang
Together. Every persons' prayer
Blew incense on the summer air, there.

*

At a point,
We opened our mouths no more.
That winter, when we shed tears again,
It was so cold they froze, and we stored them,
For water in the summer droughts.

To the Beach

Down went the lad to the beach
With the soft porn furtively smuggled
In his back-pack, stuffed deep down
In his shirt-front, crinkling it out.
The lazy waves drew in coldly,
  Too nude to care.

The huge blue sky was a blank,
No artwork there bar creation,
Itself believed by science
Which all things curve. A wench urinated,
The marram-grass shifted gently,
  The sands rippled.

He longed for love; such love as the century
Had clean forgot at its ending;
Love of a parent; hair of
A dog; love of turbot or bass;
Merman's maid the wavy brine
  Just might wash up.

He opened the bit near the back
Where girls lift their T-shirts giggling
And a bald male smirks loudly
In his shorts. The sea undulated.
The lad's nipples bulged his specs
  At their breasts' eyes.

Student Vacation

I remember Laugharne and
That undulating slag-heap of cockle-shells
Each eaten of its core and salt,
Clinging to the trees like encrusting fog,
 The mud's bog

Gleaming stenchingly beside
My adapted laundry-van where like
Jonah I encamped three days
And three nights. The square fields
 Where no one builds

Draped out to dry on the hillside
Were lovely – but not in a shout of the friendly
Stretch of unstopped sand, vast shore,
Estuary tapering to a horizontal sword
 Of light and word

Like shark-neon; as bright
As the glint of the four mackerel placed
On my driver's seat by this git from last night,
Some jokey net-repairman wanker
 I'd met in the "Dog and Anchor"

(Or whatever that hostelry was called)
Who'd lately come trawling ashore.
He took this town apart. O that's
A fact, with his under-effing-milky-
 Wood girls and their silky

Hair this sage told me. Like beer
Sea lapped in the runnels of sand,
Worrying each other in and out of the shoals.
Mice running in and out of their holes.
 Ash leaves wuthering around.

TV Time

They are all visualists.
Language is ending now.
Pouring seed out on the ground
Amidst the melting snow.

Screens are the dwelling-place,
We are projected there.
Human children come on film.
Are nothing till they are.

The galaxy's a mind.
The "living universe"
Is really little more than myth.
The planet's feral course.

For forty thousand years
A mammal crept the shore.
It scraped the sand with fingernails.
Our only future's there.

No aeons block the oaks.
Explore all parts of space,
And still a single lateral step
Returned you perfect grace.

The aborted baby smiled.
Its tiny, silent singing
Ended in a far trash can.
Love was its first thing.

Only a moment left
To cool this August sun.
A midnight knock below his lamp
Empowered that ergaton.

They are a crowd, a crowd.
The problem is
That all the teeming nests of ants
Liked blowing that to pieces

Where we inhabit surface.
Where water meets but air,
Air earth, air water, water earth,
The simple biosphere

That gendered everyman
At scratch-points on its way
Where the helium city grew itself
Only to live and die

In chlorophyll and turquoise;
These the four large gates –
Instant message, melting speed,
Climate-change and birthrates —

To go through. So to dream
Of this some aeons hence
Is a raindrop dangling on a gate
In the billion-year dance.

Fable

She was too awkward and her big nose
Turned in on itself like a whelk. At the end
Of it was a shining drop as though
Ridiculing her more symmetrical tears, yet unimpressed
By the body she had to move about in she said
Nothing, worked away at her mother's home and
School lessons, watched the sun vainly jabbing at
The filthy windows and occasionally swiped at
The dusty salt that trickled on her cheek like a fly.

In cheap dresses she stood at parties waiting
For the clatter of forks to end, men's fat and
Women's shining bums keep still and everyone go home.
She would stare for whole minutes at the corner
Of a rosewood table or scarlet napkin still folded.
The music plunked on. Other girls then students then
Adults asked her opinions and found them clear if dull.
A maniac shrieked inside her when it was not playing
With its green dolphins as she told it to.

She learned new office skills wanting no more education
Than the two degrees she completed, graduating dressed
In a flapping heavy gown and ill-suited beads, taste
Wrong but unnoticed, simply knowing where she stood.
An oaf who had spoken to her on occasion
In the lunch break on her first job then asked her
To attend a political meeting with him. They did,
Sitting side by side like concrete pillars in an
Evergreen and formal garden none of their type could
                                                        afford.

Her escort's mouth that night was like her own
Ironic navel, again she felt born hardly considered
If not actually despised. The same man
Took her out to a restaurant, they had steaks
Like grey books and gateau from the trolley sticky
And spongy as her self-image. The tab came folded,
Her inward smile questioning not what she was
Worth but how her friend's duties met his arrangements
For economy and a careful year.

Finally on a club picnic he sat next to her
On the grass wearing, believe this or not,
His pin-stripe suit smelling of sweat and chalk
And armpits. He told her he could offer
Stability and prudence, two chairs and not loneliness
At nights in the necessary silence. He had no
Playfulness or wit yet admired those things, most
Deeply, and that was how it was. With thanks
To something and him she said she would live with him.

After a quick wedding he confessed the impotence
She had suspected but pulled the eiderdown
Over her side, went out enough to encourage
Her pride in him and flicker of the heart.
One day they found unexpectedly they were both
Staring at each other at the same instant of time.
When that rough resulting coitus was over he seemed
To look at her sideways with rolled eyeballs like a dog,
Bewildered by the game or still disbelieving its master.

He was all concern in the confinement
And birth itself. The baby became boy, youth, young man
And man. It and then he was strong and
Contemplative, and agreed by all to be handsome
By virtue solely of size, virtue and thought.
Clients and colleagues behind his back admired him,
Evaluating him and with true interest assessing him,
Till he made millions, national news, and the peak of his
                                        profession.
Never had parents hoped to conceive such gratitude.

Reader, if you ask why you're being told all this,
I can only say it suddenly came in a rush
As though the computer itself had programmed urgency.
If only, like an hourglass, one could upend inadequacy
To drift, slide, spiral back where it came from. And look at
Their son? Anyone can be happy it seems, if the dice
Roll out their way and genes, intuition and sunlight
Come through the right day on the calendar.
Actually it was the son who told me this story.

Metaphysics

A loud knocking at the door.
  All looked up; all four.

One said, must be the wind.
  Branch of an oak rapping against
  The porch outside.

Another: there's no wind at all! That hinge
  Worked loose again, and when you jumped
  It set the fanlight rattling.

A third: there was no knocking.
  Isn't it all in our minds? Thought
  Is over-stimulating us tonight.

The fourth: there's a person out there.
  It sounded intended,
  That knocking air.

Blankly the other three stare.
  But there's no one in the world, they said,
  Bar us. Just we four there.

The World of Sea-Shells

The world of sea-shells.
Yes, I bend over and peer at them
But see mainly my creasing face and

No crab even as I scuttle sideways
Into age. The wind blows and
Dunes rustle, air smells so

Salt but we all know how
It isn't the same. Landscapes
Curving now, we may end with

A planet cloning ours green
As jade, blue as whales and on it
Everyone we loved in hundreds.

Spaces to avail again,
Spaces we were ferried from,
Spaces bright with unwrecked rain.

Hurry up Please, it's Time

They saved the rain in butts; took pulp and jars
To the new recycling plant; they halved
Their electricity and bore the single bulb
Of a furtive lamp; they adapted the car
To clean-fuel specification. They grew carrots
And turned the Sunday papers into compost.
They walked or bicycled instead of drove;
They put on heavy sweaters and thick
Socks and thus cut down their central heating.
They considered the lilies, how they grew,
And read their secondhand books, still wondering
If even Solomon's wisdom could suffice
To save the human venture that began
In Eden; its art, its buildings and its law.

But I can't tell you how this all worked out;
Its hour had not yet come; only
The unaborted children who survive
Will know of that, staring at their hands
Like monkeys, asking what to do next.

Eros

23 April, 1995

Valley of the Usk, exactly mid-distant
From the road; beautifully wrapped in its fields;
Sheep like bees in the evening. Mazy light.
The Usk is surprisingly deep by Llansantfraedd
Bridge, where its water swivels round the pilings.
On the lush meadow cows munched heavily.
I left at dusk for the four-hour slog.

Piccadilly. Midnight radio: "A new biography
Of Henry Vaughan....tell us about him, here
On his hillside." Squads of neon march overhead.
In the middle, on a stone knoll, love's statue
Opens its wings but never flies, the perennial
Bush for town foxes. To wheel us forward,
A glade of traffic lights, each with its green leaf.

The Picture

for SD

I knew already she had twins. Grown adults
Now, the time's duplicity achieved.
Her tribute to compassion's stealth.

Twin peaks, twin towns, twin-screw
Propellers, boats built all for speed. Bruce Chatwin
Studied them; he was intrigued, some say,
By the final letters of his name.

When I entered her room, her college room,
I saw the bulletin board, arranged with snaps
Of family and friends. In one, two children,
Cream-white tops and turquoise shorts. Identical hair,
Identical clothes, identical faces.

She took a mite to sort it.
"Oh no....well, that's Grace, just one of them —
But amused, on seeing herself
In a huge mirror!"

It was, I suppose, a species
Of epistemological thrill. No glass
Can beam identity. No two persons
Are the same. The reflected child its other child.
Two things to see. The same one twice to see.

One turns away. One is, or plucks, the rose.
One sleeps essential solitude.
There is no love bar separation.
And feel oneself more truly and more strange.

Wake up, she said, gently. *You're miles away.*

The Birdwatcher

for Lucy Newlyn

A priest as well, and his hair blew about
Like a halo, his dog-collar a choke.
He preferred the moor for walks, but hedges,
Ditches, and the muddy ruts of a wet
Field in autumn could find him too,
On occasion. He liked that solitude.

Once, caught in a chance meeting,
I tried to impress. "Ponies on the bryn
Last week, an otter in the sea. And something
Odd on the cliff; a crow with red legs –
Was it? But the locals are bored
With all that now, they've gone so global."

No reaction; as if hearing wild hoof-beats.
"Sounds like a chough" he said, drily.
"They enter their nests direct, like bullets.
Then leave free-falling. Surprised you saw it.
I've seen some. But all best things are rare."
He walked away, still determined for sky.

Hindsight on the Millennium

The planet ambled on its path,
The humans hurried to the north,
The cold Pole crackled underneath.
All circling its solar worth.

The house collapsed. Foundations rose
At angles round the splintered stairs,
The holocausts of broken glass.
Dead bodies lay on all the floors.

Amid the dust, on an armchair,
Was perched the fragile century
Which flew off like a butterfly
Out through the window and away

Right up the hillside. All survived
Who filmed it, and a few perceived
How electronically unnerved
Were the last witnesses, just saved

By being born so late. All well:
They turned to count the damage-toll,
The smashed beds, china, bathroom pearl,
Still waiting for a miracle.

Ageing

for S

I said *I love you* but you only said
how the wind was blowing the leaves around
this October. But as by then I was also saying
I love you again, I could only hope
that those words too might fly on the wind
flung safely like leaves unheard – or else maybe
waft into yourself, and plant their seed
in your sachet of earth like a sycamore key,
leaving a small tree-child in there,
or at least be conceived, not just in my mind
with its golden, hopeless, if autumn love.

A Walking Shadow

```
    h        s           I
      e              y      i

    h      h s         I?    a
  T    e  e        r   y-    ie

Wh   s th s?   h r a   I? a
T    se f el s,     o r b  y- my life?

Wha  s thi s? Wh re a  I? I  a ?
T   se f el s,your body – my life?

What is this? Where am I? I am?
These fields, your body – my life?

                    *


Yes but a black red lump touches
my body and the sun goes dark.

Ys but a lack  ed lum  to h s
m bo y an t  e  s n goe  dar .

  e b t a la k ed lu    t  hs
m  o y n t e s   g e  dar

  e   t  ak          t     s
m   yn   s    e    a

  e   t   k          t
    y        s     e
```

All Objects of All Thought

He had opposed the return of
Helen to fair-headed Menelaos%%
"3£0^67%$ who survived, when what
worked to break down the great
Wall of the Achaians. [*] [*] [*]
we truly say is translated88—++
\ \:&7592? there's a question qu

estion marque for you. Imploding
earth centripetal forces yet
eccentric in physeeeek and....
 (even today ive just heard now,
electronic barons buy the world,
+%$£7\?8@~****zszs.zszs.zszs.zsx
every last thing shown in the Louvre

is owned as to production rights
in perpetuo by a single ——=-=—
ffffffffffffhhhhhhwwwwww333333)
is reproducing you see bbbbb^^^^
investing in possible outc——ss
iiiiiiiiiiiiiiiiiiiiiiiiiiiiiiiiiiiiiiiiiiiiiiii
infinitely repeated. (NOW APPLY

REPEATER for so *Wall of the Ach*
aians. we truly say is translat
ed88—++ //:&7592? There's a END
OF REPEATER but the instant print
overrides, my time and your time,
our time and their time, a very fine
or gossamic cloud seals the earth

at the projections on the outworks,
and broke down the battlements,
and both feet beneath me are swept
and Paris struck him by the jaw
and ear, and the life spirit fled
away, out of his limbs %%%%%%%%
and hateful dark closed about him.

Green trees, green sacred planet,
grown far from yourself and diseased, so
gone near mad with your keepers'
greed and grief, each orbiting
gyration tracked by techniques
earth's energies it**self en-ge[
de(r%ed**, we^ arr oanli elec$-t-rr

Currents

Exe

Wye

                (4th bridge)

Dee

                       Tees

               m m m m m m
               m m m m m m

             the rain it raineth

Vespers of a Peasant

FRIDAY
  we are in bed
  a roof over our head
  our bodies like two dogs touch for comfort
  our boy fast asleep
  it's the bayonets, starving, fortune they are somewhere else
  tonight the evil one is kept away
  I am stupefied, I don't know what to say

SATURDAY
  we are in bed
  a roof over our head
  our bodies like two dogs touch for comfort
  our boy fast asleep
  it's the bayonets, starving, fortune they are somewhere else
  tonight the evil one is kept away
  I am stupefied, I don't know what to say

SUNDAY
  we are in bed
  a roof over our head
  our bodies like two dogs touch for comfort
  our boy fast asleep
  it's the bayonets, starving, fortune they are somewhere else
  tonight the evil one is kept away
  I am stupefied, I don't know what to say

MONDAY
  we are in bed
  a roof over our head
  our bodies like two dogs touch for comfort
  our boy fast asleep
  it's the bayonets, starving, fortune they are somewhere else
  tonight the evil one is kept away
  I am stupefied, I don't know what to say

TUESDAY
  we are in bed
  a roof over our head
  our bodies like two dogs touch for comfort
  our boy fast asleep
  it's the bayonets, starving, fortune they are somewhere else
  tonight the evil one is kept away
  I am stupefied, I don't know what to say

WEDNESDAY

Instants

imp
impious
imply

angry beauty
green sky
silver height

let's death him
once below a time
she is all fools

they could drink time
he was very married
we went on falling upwards

and Adam said I must work
and Eve said I must minister
and the serpent gave a bad apple
and God said it was good

light drizzle
torrential rain
fine weather
heavy storms
high winds

Mary's eyes are red
Mary's eyes are blue

> *the hammer hammered and the comb combed,*
> *the inventor invented and the talker talked*
> *the sweep swept but with no hazel birch,*
> *and never once the iron spade stopped pounding*

The Matter

take away that
lamp-standard, *take*
away that table, *take*
away those
chairs. *take away*
that carpet. *take*
away that dresser
and *take away* the
row of plates
along it. *take away*
the fire-guard and
the coal, *take away*
the bowl of fruit, *take*
away the cigarette-
box and the cigarette
ends in the ashtray
next to it. *take*
away that empty
coffee cup. *take*
away that light,
that upturned book and
pencil with the
sharpened point, and
the ballpoint. *take*
away the record-
player and sleeves and
groove. *take away*
the curtains. *take*
away that vase.
take away the ceiling,
and *take away* the
hanging light. *take*
away the floor. *take*
away the four walls

and the pictures.
take away the
air and the particles
of dust, the molecules of
smell in the air. *take
away* the matter,
take away the air's
energy. then take
away *take away*

Ballad

o sonn ma mongol chile
nice cloas u ware tday
lk u so smart bin al things smart
for on so special day

o mama wer r we?
doan wan stay hom tday
go out to fiels, stream, big dark wd.
world is oh plas to play

were gong den a big ride.
daddo is draving day
o mama o is fun dis ride
und us go hom for tay.

a mam were do we go?
dad drive sa far to day
here am de trees al green is fine.
wy doan stay here to play?

o son my torturd chile
we drive in car tday.
doan ask no qestion, dad do rite,
smile at the sky des way.

o mom dat splend ad hous
can we stap heer so gay
o now me kno we cam heare why,
car stap. get aut u say.

o chile my mongrl chile
yes brought u thus tday.
we pray so hard, now lk this son,
step down watch now i say.

o mam i knu so fore
world hav luv tings dis way
u muth so gud an father gd.
wy leav heer now tday?

o chile o mangle chile
see laidy heare so gay.
shee spik so nice and lik u does.
o boy mine boy dis way.

o man wu dis wo man?
o nice dis place i say.
u me an dad wil come dis place
to see de place so gay?

o chile ma mangle chile
now hear now wat we say
glad a yu like dis place so well
now so dt we cn stay.

o mam u like dis place?
o man now yes u say
o mam why dad he luk me so
when u sed yes we stay.

o chile my own gull chile
time now we drahv away
o chile de good lorde hav u here
dis wo man giv u gay.

o mam wat u me done?
o mam how cam dis day?
nat leav me mam, wat i don wrong
dat u mus goon away!

o chile my own my chile
to be gd, so god say.
we leve u chile who don no wrong.
dat wy we go away.

o man man wat u don
dis chile dform dis way?
an dis pore modder leav her chile
how say u lor dis day?

What is Life

what is life?
  ha

thought
  ugh

love
 o

*

like a t e w ves ma e toward the ebbled shore
so do our minutes h sten to thei nd

    s h   a   ke   s   pe
           a   r e

*

TOURISM IS LEISURE
  o u r   i s l e

Acknowledgements

Magazines, journals and radio

Acumen, Anglo-Welsh Review, Aquarius, Bête Noire, Critical Quarterly, English, The Frogmore Papers, The Independent, The Interpreter's House, London Magazine, London Welshman, Magma, New Poetry, New Welsh Review, Other Poetry, Outposts, Planet, P N Review, Poetry Australia, Poetry Chicago (USA), Poetry Durham, Poetry London, Poetry Nottingham, Poetry Review, Poetry Wales, The Rialto, Scintilla, Spectrum, Staple, Swansea Review, Thumbscrew, Times Literary Supplement, Transatlantic Review, Tribune, The Use of English, Webster Review (USA), Western Mail, Workshop New Poetry and BBC Radio 3 and 4, and BBC Radio Wales.

Anthologies

Anglo-Welsh Poetry 1480-1980 (Poetry Wales Press, 1984), A Poet's 1982 (Poet & Printer), Best of the Poetry Year (Robson, 1979), Burning the Bracken (Seren, 1996), The Bright Field (Carcanet, 1991), Chatter of Choughs (Oxford: St Edmund Hall/Signal Books, 2001), Earth Songs (Green Books, 2002), The Forward Book of Poetry (Forward, 1993), Green Horse (Christopher Davies Ltd., 1978), Hero's Way: Contemporary Poets in the Mythic Tradition (Prentice-Hall, USA), The Hutchinson Book of Post-War British Poets (Hutchinson, 1989) Picture: Welsh Poets (Gwent/Seren), Poems of the Decade (Forward, 2001), Poems '76 (Gomer, 1976), Poems for Radio (Enitharmon, 2002) Poetry South East (South East Arts, 1982), Poetry Wales: 25 Years (Seren, 1990), The River's Voice (Green Books 2000), A Swansea Anthology (Seren, 1996), Twentieth Century Anglo-Welsh Poetry (Seren, 1997), Wales: An Anthology (Collins, 1989), Wales in Verse (Secker & Warburg, 1983) and Writers Review Yearbook (1971).

Three poems in the final section of the book appeared in my exhibition Poetry or Type, shown at the Foyer Gallery, University of Swansea (1981), the Kent Literature Festival in Folkestone (1992) and the Cardiff Literature Festival (1993).

'Still Life' and 'Calvin' appeared in a small pamphlet, Things, Bran's Head Press (1981). 'Before Experience' appeared as a Sceptre Press Broadsheet in 1974.